OTHER BOOKS BY LES PARROTT III

Seven Secrets of a Healthy Dating Relationship
Saving Your Marriage Before It Starts: Seven Questions to Ask Before (and After) You Marry (with Leslie Parrott)
Becoming Soul-Mates: Cultivating Spiritual Intimacy in the Early Years of Marriage (with Leslie Parrott)
Questions Couples Ask (with Leslie Parrott)
The Marriage Mentor Manual (with Leslie Parrott)
High Maintenance Relationships: How to Handle Impossible People
Love's Unseen Enemy: How to Overcome Guilt to Build Healthy Relationships
Helping the Struggling Adolescent: A Guide to Thirty Common Problems for Parents, Counselors, and Youthworkers
Helping the Struggling Adolescent: A Counseling Guide
The Career Counselor: Guidance for Planning Careers and Managing Career Crises (with Leslie Parrott)

SOUND RECORDINGS AND VIDEO RECORDINGS BY LES PARROTT III

7 Secrets of a Healthy Dating Relationship, videocassette
Escaping the Guilt Trap, AACC, videocassette
Saving Your Marriage Before It Starts (with Leslie Parrott), videocassette
Saving Your Marriage Before It Starts (with Leslie Parrott), audiocassette

Once Upon a Family

Building a Healthy Home
When Your Family
Isn't a Fairy Tale

Les Parrott III

Beacon Hill Press of Kansas City
Kansas City, Missouri

Copyright 1996
by Beacon Hill Press of Kansas City

ISBN 083-411-5972

Continuing Lay Training Unit 420.04A

Printed in the
United States of America

Cover Design: Ted Ferguson
Cover Photo: Third Coast Stock Source Inc.

Library of Congress Cataloging-in-Publication Data
Parrott, Les.
    Once upon a family : building a healthy home when your family
isn't a fairy tale / Les Parrott III.
        p.   cm.
    Includes bibliographical references.
    ISBN 0-8341-1597-2 (pbk.)
    1. Family—United States. 2. Marriage—United States. 3. Family—Religious aspects—Christianity.   I. Title.
HQ536.P373   1996
306.85'0973—dc21   96-44598
                                                                      CIP

10   9   8   7   6   5   4   3   2   1

In memory of my grandparents—
Alonzo Leslie and Lucile Parrott
James W. and Lora Montgomery

Contents

Acknowledgments

Several people have been a vital part of this project. My thanks to to Hardy Weathers for bringing this idea to me. Bob Brower and Mike Estep offered unflinching confidence in my ability to write this book. Mark Brown and Kelly Gallagher assisted me in numerous ways to make this process easier. Paul Martin made many helpful suggestions and gave careful editorial attention to the book. The whole Beacon Hill Press team played an important role in making this book what it is.

Special thanks go to friends and colleagues who contributed sidebar material for this book: Joe Bentz, Samuel L. Dunn, Leola Floren, Fred Fullerton, Mark Gilroy, Miriam J. Hall, Grace Ketterman, Tom Nees, John A. Knight, Ed Robinson, Wesley D. Tracy, and Steve Weber.

It would contradict the message of this book if I did not take this opportunity to thank my family: Mom and Dad, Rich and Carol, Roger and Mary Lou, Andrew, Justin, Grady, Madison, and of course, Leslie. I love you all more than you will ever know.

The Family and the Bible

One does not have to be a Judeo or Christian believer to acknowledge the tremendous moral and spiritual depth of the Old and New Testaments and their powerful impact on Western civilization. Past president Dwight D. Eisenhower of the United States observed, "The purpose of a devout and united people was set forth in the pages of the Bible."

Another past president of the United States, Herbert C. Hoover, commented, "The whole inspiration of our civilization springs from the teachings of Christ and the lessons of the prophets. To read the Bible for these fundamentals is a necessity of American life."

Ulysses S. Grant, an earlier president than the two just cited, admonished, "Hold fast to the Bible as the sheet anchor of your liberties; write its precepts in your hearts, and practice them in your lives. To the influence of this Book are we indebted for all the progress made in true civilization, and to this must we look as our Guide in the future."

Most would concur that the family unit is the backbone, the heart and soul, of any society. The moral principles advanced by the Bible have been brought to bear on Western culture largely through the family. Apart from these guidelines and teachings both the family and the entire society begin the process of dissolution and disintegration.

The family has been properly called "the giant shock absorber of society," the one stable point in a flux-filled culture. Homes are important, because what goes on in the homes of the world today will go on in the world tomorrow. The value of the Bible with its message of love and right relationships cannot be overestimated in strengthening the family and bringing stability and justice to all of society.

John A. Knight

1

In the Beginning God Created Families

Call it a clan, call it a network, call it a tribe,
call it a family. Whatever you call it,
whoever you are, you need one.

—Jane Howard

ABOUT 1,000 PEOPLE WRITE TO HER EVERY DAY. SHE HAS EIGHT secretaries and two clerks who sift the letters down to about 200, sorting them into categories. Each letter tells a story and then asks questions of a woman who has spent more than 40 years dispensing advice to the lonely, afflicted, battered, diseased, and confused: Ann Landers. "The changes I have seen," she once wrote, "would twirl your turban."[1] Over the years her advice has shifted from bad breath to AIDS (acquired immune deficiency syndrome), from spoiled brats to gun-toting 10-year-olds. Despite the changes, Ann says the number one issue people have questions about is families. "It's always been that way," she observes, "and I suspect it's always going to be that way."

How could it be otherwise? Within the family our personhood and identity take shape. Our family provides us with a blueprint for ways of being. From our family we learn rules, regulations, and expectations about behavior. In the family setting we learn about what kinds of feelings are acceptable, appropriate, and tolerable. Almost every subject is taught in the family, from politics to religion, from psychology to philosophy—and, of course, Christianity.

John Wesley once said, "I learned more about Christianity from my mother than from all the theologians of England." Lessons are learned at home more quickly than any university professor could ever hope for in a classroom. These become the foundation on which our thinking, our motives, and our personality are formed. No wonder Ann Landers gets more questions about the family than any other subject!

And it's no wonder either that God designed human beings to live in families. Throughout human history the family has fulfilled God's intent to provide a setting for creation and care. "Ordained of God as the basic unit of human organization," writes Charles Colson, "the family is the first school of human instruction." Colson couldn't be more right. We learn most everything from our families. That's the way God made it.

The Way We Were

In the early years of our country, home was central to every important function and event in the family. Birthdays and holidays were celebrated at home. The dining room table featured Mother's favorite menus and recipes. In many homes Sunday dinner was the biggest occasion of the week. No one ever thought of going out to a hotel dining room for a family celebration, because anything worthwhile was enjoyed at home.

Divorces were rare in those days because of family economic dependence. All the members of the family needed each other, and they accepted that fact. This was true not just for the immediate family but extended family as well; Grandma and Grandpa, aunts and uncles, nephews and nieces were often a vital part of the typical home.

For most North American families, the local school had a

central place of importance. School boards consisted of parents whose children were enrolled in the school. One-room schoolhouses served as landmarks invested with great emotional content.

The local church also enjoyed a close tie to the family. Sometimes the schoolhouse served as both a center for learning on weekdays and as a church meetinghouse on Sundays. There was one thing, however, the church never did for the family: It never assumed the responsibility of Christian education. Each family saw to it that their children learned the great stories of the Bible. They often memorized important passages of Scripture.

History tells us, however, that change was on the way. The automobile was invented, and with its arrival the family shifted gears. Almost overnight this new mobility made the home less important. As more and more ribbons of concrete crisscrossed our nation, hotels and restaurants appeared on the landscape. Young people who formerly courted with adults near at hand were suddenly, by a set of wheels, cut loose from all supervision. In a matter of minutes they could go places where only their own conscience and sense of responsibility were left to guide them.

What the automobile had begun the assembly line completed. Power-driven machinery and the development of factory automation created a large increase in production of many kinds of goods. People began to leave their handmade way of life. They moved away from the farms and into the cities to work in these modern factories. They lived as close to the factories as they could; and when there was no more space, they began to stack their houses on top of each other. The high-rise was born.

Industrialization changed the Western world from a basically agricultural society to an urban society. It brought many material benefits, but, for better or worse, it also changed family life forever. In the urban lifestyle, for example, economic advancement had to do with getting the job done efficiently. Thus, status was now based on performance, not family heritage. This also meant that family members were no longer as dependent on one another for economic survival.

As family life entered the 1950s, television entered our homes with programs like *Ozzie and Harriet* and *Father Knows Best*. They mirrored the suburban lifestyle many families idealized. The relatively low divorce rate at this time seemed to confirm the impression that families' problems were fairly happy ones and could be solved before the end of a 30-minute sitcom. It was also during this decade that the baby boom began.

In the 1960s we wanted a revolution, and we got it! In contrast to the pro-marriage attitude of the '50s, the late '60s became a tumultuous time for families. With the availability of the pill, new lifestyles like living together without marriage became an issue. It became hip to disregard marriage and family. Hundreds of articles and books appeared with titles such as *The Crisis of the Nuclear Family, Is Marriage Necessary?* and *Is Monogamy Outdated?* In 1970 the book *Death of the Family* was widely read.

The "me decade" of the '70s brought more changes affecting family life. During this time we became interested in anything that began with *self*: self-esteem, self-acceptance, self-assertion, self-enhancement, and so on. Bookstores were filled with titles such as *I'm OK, You're OK; Pulling Your Own Strings; Looking Out for Number One;* and *I Just Met Someone I Like and It's Me.* By 1979 the divorce rate was 147 percent higher than in the 1960s.

The '80s reverberated from the shifts that began in those turbulent decades. In this decade "solutions" to better family life showed up in increasing numbers of working mothers, more single-parent families, unwed mothers, and an ever-soaring divorce rate. Without doubt, the recent years have given families a bumpy road to travel. Indeed, this road has brought us to the precipice of the 21st century.

The Way We Are

With only 3 percent of the population in the United States living on farms, many aspects of rural lifestyles have disappeared. Home, the center of everything important, has become little more than a Grand Central Station we pass through en route to some place more important. When *USA Today* asked teens and grown-ups about their most important possession, they both agreed: their car.[2] For most families, home has become a place to go when there is nothing more exciting to do. And when we are home, most families are watching one of their three television sets. Some studies report that in most homes televisions are turned on an average of seven hours each day.

It could be argued that television brought us together in the '50s. There were evenings when families seemed glued to the same show—Milton Berle's program or *I Love Lucy* or, yes, *Ozzie and Harriet*. Cable television, however, has had quite the opposite effect. It often divides audiences into demographic slivers. The choices are exhilarating but also alienating. It has become far more difficult to sustain a sense of family community and common values.

Even such a thing as children's play is different today. Sandlot baseball is seldom needed anymore. We are organized with Little Leagues that provide adultlike competition on an organized basis. We seldom cook a big dinner at home because too many restaurants make it easier to eat out. Long ago husbands brought home the bacon, and wives cooked it. Not today. Only 22 percent of married-couples households contain a male breadwinner and a female homemaker, a dramatic decline from 61 percent in 1960. A new division of labor has taken place, reinforced by the closing gap between men's and women's earnings.

Research suggests that these changes are affecting families in several ways. First, the increasing number of divorces and single-parent families today can be attributed *in part* to the lack of economic dependence that has been part of North American families over time. People who can support themselves and their children have less need to depend on each other. As economic changes replace communal values with individual ones, the family life span shortens, and people have fewer children. Of course, raising children is one function that usually characterizes the family—and it still does; but with divorce and unwed mothers, it is more and more likely to occur in the absence of marriage.

Back to the Future?

Do all these shifts, trends, and changes mean that family is on its way out? Not if you believe what many people say about their values. In survey after survey, traditional relationships among parents, children, and siblings are identified as the most important aspect of life. Families are seen as more important than work, recreation, friendships, or status. The truth is that researchers have been asking us about our families for over half a century, and we have always replied that the family takes priority over everything else in our lives.

The problem now is that many continue to say they embrace traditional family values—but their family relations have changed dramatically. We say traditional families are important, but on the whole our behavior doesn't show it. Traditional family relationships are in definite trouble. The family of the 21st century isn't going to look anything like the rural, farm-based family of long ago or even the family of the '50s.

The earthshaking changes our society has experienced in recent decades impact every family today. No one is exempt from the aftershocks. However, in spite of these changes, many families are holding on to tradition. Many of those families who have been fragmented are working diligently to recover all that they can. Perhaps the reports of the death of the family have been exaggerated. We cannot afford to keep ourselves from celebrating the success of many committed families—sometimes different in form—who are fulfilling God's design for creation and care.

Gary Collins, author of the book *Family Shock,* states, "The Bible never gives any indication that families—nuclear-biological and extended families—are passé." While the function, structure, and shape of some families are changing, the family's importance has not diminished. No matter what powerful changes occur in society, we will always need the love of a family. We will always desire the warmth of home and hearth. The family is a durable institution. As it is pulled and pushed in these changing times, we must keep our eyes focused on God's call to make our families Christ-centered. As Oswald Chambers once wrote, "The greatest benefits God has conferred on human life, fatherhood, motherhood, childhood, home, become the greatest curse if Jesus Christ is not the head."

Henry Drummond understood the same thing when he said, "The family circle is the supreme conductor of Christianity." Let us remember: In the beginning God created families, and families have no hope without God.

Questions for Reflection

- When you think of your family, of whom do you think? Make a list of those who are in your family.
- What is your picture of the ideal family from history and your ideal picture of the family today? Do they differ?
- What trend or fact about today's families is most disturbing to you?
- Considering all of the societal change affecting families today, do you tend to look at the glass as half full or half empty? In other words, are you optimistic or pessimistic about the American family's future?

Families Across Cultures

Realizing the stress and strain of normal family life, how much more difficult that challenge becomes when the family crosses major cultural boundaries! Imagine attempting all the normal activities of your day, but having the additional challenge of functioning in another language, within another worldview, and an entirely new set of social values.

I have lived and worked cross-culturally for nearly three decades. I have experienced and observed numerous examples of both successful and not-so-successful families attempting to adapt to the process of assimilating another culture. There are many words that could describe families of cross cultures. However, the word *flexibility* is highest on my list. Without the ability to adapt, to become and to remain flexible, the family is headed for serious trouble in this area of living cross-culturally.

Whether the culture literally changes all around you (such as through immigration, changing neighborhoods, and so on), or you move purposely into another cultural setting, the ability to become flexible is critically important. Specifically, the skill of "getting inside the other guy's skin" is to be able to see things from another completely different perspective. This allows the family of cross cultures to engage upon a successful transition to the host culture.

To a certain degree we all face the challenge of managing cultural diversity. It is imperative that we face this challenge with a huge dose of flexibility.

Steve Weber

2

Is the Family an Endangered Species?

Whoever said that death and taxes
are the only inevitable things in life
was overlooking an obvious third one: family.
—William J. Doherty

ACCORDING TO SOME, THE FAMILY HAS BEEN "IN DECLINE" SINCE the beginning of history. Yet during the past 25 years decline in modern family life has been both steeper and more alarming than during any other quarter century in our history. Experts describe the transformation of this period with terms such as "dramatic," "revolutionary," and "unparalleled." The family meltdown recently caused the American Psychological Association to rate "the decline of the nuclear family" as today's number one threat to mental health.

It's the baby-boom generation's family years, but the boomerang isn't returning. Married couples with children are fading fast as a share of all households. And as the children of older baby boomers leave home, the share of traditional families will erode even further. Are we witnessing the end of an epoch? Is the American family an endangered species?

Unless dramatic, revolutionary, and unparalleled measures are taken quickly, the deafening answer is *yes*. Sound the alarm! The two-parent family and its children are in trouble.

The Splintered American Family

A latter-day Norman Rockwell would be hard-pressed to paint today's "typical family." Consider the choices: childless couples, unmarried live-togethers, single-parent households, divorced parents who share custody, even gay couples who adopt children. George Barna's research depicts the average American family these days as consisting of a married couple with one child, in which both parents are employed. At least one of the parents is likely to have been divorced. Less than half of all children born today will live continuously with both biological parents throughout childhood. They will spend several years in a single-parent family. Some will eventually live in blended, stepparent families. (Chapter 10 of this book is devoted to these families.)

The soaring divorce rate of today's marriages is two to three times what it was for our parents and grandparents. About half of all who currently marry will divorce within seven years. Divorce has become so widespread that many scholars are beginning to view it as part of the normal life course of American marriages.

For some, marriage is no longer an institution but a path toward self-fulfillment. It becomes a relationship to make and break at will. In the not-too-distant future, according to Barna, many individuals will generally believe that a life spent with the same partner is both unusual and unnecessary. "Serial monogamy," in which one chooses a partner who will best satisfy his or her needs during a specific period of his or her life, is becoming the norm. Lifelong commitments are dying. Marriage is on the verge of becoming only a temporary union.

The Perilous Consequences

The effects of divorce span generations. The first generation of children for whom divorced parents were commonplace are now becoming adults, and they are a new breed. Children of divorce leave home earlier than others, but not to form families of their own. They are far more likely than their peers to cohabit before they marry, and once they do marry, they are also more likely to divorce.

Cohabiting households, by the way, can look like a traditional family from the outside, but on the inside they function differently than married couples' households. Cohabiting couples share the housework more equitably than married couples, but they share child care less. The children usually belong to and are cared for by the woman.

The withering family affects more than couples. Its consequences are seen in people of all ages. Over the last three decades, for example, older parents have been less likely to live with their adult children and more likely to live alone. They are less likely to find comfort from their children. Today's high divorce rates mean that many fathers now spend little time with their young children. And research shows that adult children spend less time and money on an elderly father if they had infrequent contact with him when they were young.

However, the greatest negative effect of recent trends, in the opinion of nearly everyone, is not on adults. It is on children. There is substantial, if not conclusive, evidence that the quality of life for children in the past 25 years has worsened. A disinvestment in family life invariably means a disinvestment in children's welfare. Some are calling the situation a national "parent deficit." Every child desires two biological parents for life. And research shows that child rearing is most successful when it involves two motivated parents. This is not to say that other family forms cannot be successful—only that as a group they are not as likely to be so.

The evidence is in, and the word is getting out. Yale psychologists Edward Zigler and Elizabeth Gilman, reporting a consensus among researchers, sum it up this way: "In the past 30 years of monitoring the indications of child well-being, never have the indicators looked so negative." A special commission on youth recently concluded, "Never before has one generation of American teenagers been less healthy, less cared for, or less prepared for life." Barbara Dafoe Whitehead, in her interesting *Atlantic Monthly* article "Dan Quayle Was Right," reports that "children in families disrupted by divorce and out-of-wedlock birth do worse than children in intact families on several measures of well-being . . . [they are more likely to] be poor . . . have emotional and behavioral problems . . . drop out of high school . . . get pregnant as teenagers . . . abuse drugs . . . get in trouble with the law."

In a recent editorial Mortimer Zuckerman, editor in chief of *U.S. News and World Report,* wrote, "The impact that family disintegration has on children's lives is a national crisis. The time for silence is over."

Sounding the Alarm

What should be done to remedy the negative effects of family decline? There are no simple solutions. The traditional nuclear family characteristic of the 1950s, however, is not the answer. Aside from the fact that it is probably impossible to return to a time when "father knew best," it has significant drawbacks. To some extent, it would require many women to become "de-liberated" and leave the workforce. Economic conditions necessitate that women have careers, not to mention that equality between the sexes is an advancement too valuable to forfeit.

By posing additional questions, David G. Myers, author and psychologist at Hope College in Holland, Michigan, answers the question of what should be done: "Can we agree that we aren't returning to the 'Father Knows Best' world of the '50s? That we now value intimate companionship and equality? That we can accept family diversity and support single parents while acknowledging the evidence that children benefit when jointly nurtured by two caring parents?"

The time is ripe for people of diverse opinion to come together with shared concerns. We cannot depend on the welfare state for a solution to the siege. Reinhold Niebuhr said, "Family life is too intimate to be preserved by the spirit of justice. It can be sustained by a spirit of love which goes beyond justice."

We need a new social movement whose purpose is the

promotion of families and their values within the new constraints of modern life. Children are getting woefully short-changed and need us to build a society of enduring families and monogamous marriages. For this reason, we must reinvigorate the cultural ideals of family within the changed circumstances of our time. We must love and support those who are single or divorced while bringing to the forefront the old ideal of parents living together and sharing responsibility for their children and for each other. Strong families concerned with the needs of children and built on biblical principles are not only possible but necessary.

William J. Bennett, former United States secretary of education, comments, "Treatises have been written on why [the decline of families] has occurred, on why we have allowed this to occur. The hard truth is that in the free society the ultimate responsibility rests with the people themselves. It is our beliefs, our behavior and our philosophy that have in many instances changed for the worst. Our injury is self-inflicted. The good news is that what has been self-inflicted can be self-restored." I couldn't agree more.

Questions for Reflection

- How would you describe the decline of the American family that has occurred the last few decades?
- Many believe that in modern times marriage has evolved into a path toward self-fulfillment. Why is this a trend that should concern the Church?
- What do you think about the idea that as a society we can never return to the traditional ideal of families in previous generations?
- What are some of the most encouraging signs you see for the family to grow stronger and healthier in the years ahead?

Number of Homes Headed by a Single Parent

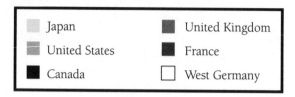

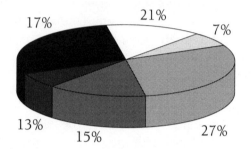

Source: United States Census Bureau

Number of Women Giving Birth Outside of Marriage
(in thousands)

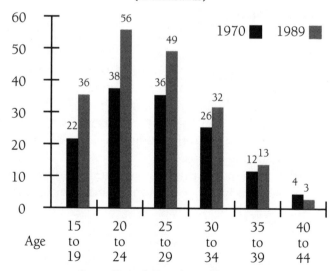

Source: National Center for Health Statistics

How Adults Define Family Values

Values	Percent
Respecting your parents	70
Providing emotional support for your family	69
Respecting people for who they are	68
Being responsible for your actions	68
Communicating your feeling to your family	65
Respecting your children	65
Having a happy marriage	64
Having faith in God	59
Respecting authority	57
Living up to your potential	54
Being married to the same person for life	54

Source: Massachusetts Mutual American Family Values Study

Family Futures

The family has traditionally been viewed as a group of persons with a lifelong commitment to each other who share love; who are committed to meeting each other's psychological, social, and spiritual needs; and who share economic resources. The central feature of the traditional family is a husband and wife who have legally and morally bound themselves to each other for life in love, for the purpose of mutual support, and to provide nurture for the children who might be born to them.

Social, economic, political, and scientific forces are now tearing that picture apart. A new picture is becoming visible, one showing a family structure very different in form and purpose. The new family consists of a group of persons who share some values and goals, have a commitment to each other for an unspecified period of time, and share resources and decisions.

In the Christian West, the ties that bound the traditional family together were woven in concert by the state, the Church, and society in general, all of which shared common foundational values. As the state has become increasingly secularized, and as a significant portion of society has lost its commitment to traditional values, the ties are weakened and torn, allowing new patterns of family practice to emerge.

Societal expectations for families and marriages in the West at the beginning of the 21st century will be very different from expectations at the beginning of the 20th. Persons who prize the traditional family will be hard-pressed to maintain those kinds of families for themselves and their children. Only a full-court press, backed by the best scholarship available, well-funded political action, and business acumen can redirect the forces leading to the new family.

Samuel L. Dunn

3

How Our Families Shape Our Lives

Sometimes you'll get so far away
from your family you'll think you're outside
its influence forever, then before you
figure out what's happening, it will be right
beside you, pulling the strings.

—Peter Collier

JULIE WAS AN INTELLIGENT, ENTHUSIASTIC WOMAN IN HER MID-20s. She invested much of her discretionary time procuring donations from area businesses in order to send shipments of toys to orphans in Romania. She had developed the contacts on her own and initiated the entire effort. When she talked about those children, her eyes lit up her entire face.

But here she was in my office, shifting uncomfortably in her chair as she talked about her stalled efforts to make a career decision. A recent college graduate, she had spent time investigating opportunities to work as a travel agent, yet nothing was falling into place. Knowing her level of business savvy and professionalism, I was surprised to hear that she wasn't able to find an entry-level position in a local travel agency. In fact, I had a growing hunch that an underlying barrier had preempted Julie's efforts.

As we talked, I began to ask exploratory questions. "Julie, who among your circle of family and friends is invested in or anxious about the outcome of your career decisions?"

"It's funny you should ask that. My father called just last night to check on the status of my job search. It didn't go very well. He gave me a long lecture, said I wasn't really trying hard. I got so upset that I hung up."

Julie unfolded the story of parents who had encouraged her to apply to travel agencies. All she could understand was that they would enjoy the availability of the free travel benefits for the whole family. The combination of their pressure and her guilt had convinced her that she owed it to them after all they had done to help her complete her education. Once this was uncovered, Julie was able to see how her efforts to obtain a position in the travel industry were failing in great part due to her own unconscious self-sabotage. Her dream was to work in a not-for-profit agency focused on the needs of Romanian orphans, and eventually to work directly in a Romanian orphanage. She didn't want to work in a travel agency—that was something her mom and dad wanted.

All of us, whether we admit it or not, are like Julie. We are shaped by our family. In fact, most of what we think, say, and do—for better or worse—is a response to the home in which we grew up. After all, the family is the first social organization with which the fledgling human being comes into contact. It is within the family that we incorporate the skills and knowledge that will one day enable us to live outside it. From the career we choose to the person we marry, from the politics we support to the values we live by, every conceivable aspect of our lives is shaped by our family. Knowingly or not, either we buy into what our family taught us, or we fight against it. What we learn with the family are the most unforgettable lessons our lives will ever teach us. As Theodor Lidz points out in *The Person,* "It is in the family that patterns of emotional reactivity develop and interpersonal relationships are established that pattern and color all subsequent relation-ships."

Experts on the family consistently point to three areas where our families' sculpting power is most powerfully present: (1) family rules, (2) family roles, and (3) family relationships.

Unspoken Family Rules

Each family has its own unique set of unspoken rules. These rules create an environment of consistency and predictability within the family structure. For example, one family may operate by the rule that everyone should get a college education. It isn't discussed, it is simply expected. Another family, on the other hand, may live by the idea that real achievement is succeeding in business without the intrusion of formal training.

While family rules may be explicit, they are more often unspoken, operating outside the conscious awareness of every family member. No one may say, "You have to get a degree," but the rule is unconsciously present. It draws strength and is formed from picking up subtle and not-so-subtle attitudes. Hearing family stories about the glory and achievement of a parent's college experience, for example, can be a way of saying, "You should do the same."

Family rules unconsciously guide individuals by describing what family members should do and how they should behave—even if they fly in the face of a person's real desires, as Julie's family's did. By the way, once Julie raised her awareness of the unspoken rules by which she was operating, the rules her family unknowingly perpetuated and instilled in her, she was more able to make conscious, intentional decisions about her career.

What about you? What unspoken rules did your family live by? Take a moment to think about this. The following sentence stems can help you uncover these rules. Simply complete them by writing the first idea that pops into your head:

- Men should . . .
- Women should . . .

- Success is . . .
- The most important thing . . .
- Life . . .

The point of uncovering your family's unspoken rules is to examine them and evaluate them from your personal perspective. Once you become aware of these powerful rules, you can choose to consciously incorporate them into your life *or* transcend them. Either way, your heightened awareness of how your family has shaped you will make you a healthier person.

Unconscious Family Roles

Jeff, a 20-something college graduate, came into my office unannounced. He had been my student a few years back, and I knew he could always be counted on for a little levity. "Hey!" I said, as he appeared at my door. "What's the joke of the day?"

Jeff didn't spark to my greeting. "No jokes today, Doc." He was notably different as we had a bit of idle conversation. Then tears began to well up in his eyes. He dropped his gaze, and we sat together silently for a few seconds. With a deep sigh, Jeff then revealed that his older brother—who had been on a fast track in a very successful career—had recently been killed in a car accident. Suddenly the happy-go-lucky Jeff, who had been content with his retail job at an outdoor equipment supplier, felt the mantle of "oldest and only son" falling on his shoulders. Now that his role in the family had changed, everything about his future looked different.

Birth order and sibling dynamics are significant factors in shaping one's role in the family. How we act has a lot to do with our family constellation—whether we are oldest or youngest, male or female, and so on. For example, siblings tend not to select the same careers but usually choose to go in different directions. The point is that roles played out within the family often develop into occupational or vocational pursuits.[1]

Jeff had crossed the professional career track off his list of options, since his older brother had chosen a profession. Jeff's role as a fun-loving, carefree youngest child had comfortably developed into a vocational choice to work with outdoor, adventure-related equipment. But the death of his brother had redefined the boundaries of Jeff's role in the family and created an identity crisis. Suddenly he looked at all of life differently. His career, his decision to put off marriage, his dreams were changing, because his perceived role in his family of origin had changed.

Have you given much thought to your role in the home you grew up in? What part did you play in your family's drama? Consider the following roles to help you more accurately pinpoint your part:

- Problem Solver
- Healer
- Victim
- Rescuer
- Comedian
- Mediator
- Confronter
- Secret-Keeper
- Other

You may also find it helpful to identify other family members' parts. This will help you more clearly define your role. So review the list again, and try to determine what role each member of your family played. By identifying your role in the family, you will become more empowered to fulfill it if you choose, or carve out a more healthful pattern if need be.

Triangles in Family Relationships

Relationships of all kinds are susceptible to temporary triangles, but families are swimming in them. A relational triangle emerges anytime a third person becomes involved in an anxious or conflictual two-person relationship.

Helen, a single woman in her mid-30s, had always dreamed of traveling abroad, and for the first time in her life she had the opportunity. In fact, she and a girlfriend from church were going to Italy for 10 weeks to work temporarily at a design studio where her friend had connections. Helen was very excited.

As a mature adult, Helen was independent, but she still lived in the same small town and attended the same church as her parents. In fact, they often enjoyed Sunday lunch together. And it was at Sunday lunch that Helen told her parents the exciting news about her trip. As it turned out, however, her parents, who had never even thought about traveling overseas, weren't so excited. Her dad asked why she would need to take such a trip, and her mother stepped in, aggressively suggesting that Helen seemed depressed and despondent. Helen couldn't believe her ears.

The next thing Helen knew, her mom had scheduled an appointment for Helen to see a psychiatrist. Her relatively uninvolved father suddenly encouraged Helen to go to the appointment. Helen endured a couple of interviews with a puzzled psychiatrist and fought her parents' escalating efforts to cancel her trip. Finally she gave in and passed up the opportunity to go abroad—and things at home with the family were serene once again.

Ironically, just as Helen was doing something she felt committed to and excited about—the very thing her family supported in theory—her parents moved in to resist it. Why?

The answer is found in a family triangle. In some families a person becomes so entrenched in a triangulated role that his or her identity cannot be separated from it. That was Helen's problem. Over the years, she had served as mediator between her mother and father. Her presence in the family helped keep the peace. And because this was a particularly bad time in her parents' relationship, they were depending on her heavily, albeit unconsciously, to absorb the stress between them. Helen's plan to leave for 10 weeks was so threatening to the family's delicate relational balance that a crisis ensued.

Eventually Helen transcended what she called the "strangulation of triangulation." She realized that as long as she continued to carry such a substantial responsibility for her parents' relationship, she would have little energy to invest in other relationships. Her role in the triangle sabotaged her attempts to develop a separate identity. Though she had missed her opportunity for study abroad, she eventually took other steps that set healthier boundaries between herself and her parents' relationship.

What about you? Do you see emotional triangles in your family? How do they impact your life today? Consider the different relationships in your family of origin, between Mom, Dad, and siblings, and determine how you may have served in a triangle to solve problems or make peace.

For some individuals, family will be an extremely empowering presence in negotiating all of life. For most, however, their families will present a mixed legacy with several hurdles to overcome. Rabbi and family therapist Edwin Friedman powerfully captures this reality in his book *Generation to Generation:*

> The position we occupy in our family of origin is the only thing we can never share or give to another while we are still alive. It is the source of our uniqueness, and hence, the basic parameter of our emotional potential as well as our difficulties. This unique position can dilute or nourish natural strengths; it can be a dragging weight that slows our progress throughout life, or an additive that enriches the mixture of our propelling fuel. The more we understand that position, therefore, and the more we can learn to occupy it with grace and "savvy," rather than fleeing from it or unwittingly allowing it to program our destiny, the more effectively we can function in any other area of our life.[2]

Questions for Reflection

- Can you think of another social force that has more power in shaping our lives than the family? Why, or why not?
- In what specific ways has your family of origin shaped your personality, your career choice, your marriage, your values?

- Of the three major ways families shape us (rules, roles, and relationships), which one do you see as the most influential, and why?
- Since the family is so powerful in shaping an individual's choices and even identity, what implications does this have for you as a parent?

A Family Without Boundaries

As a white person in an African-American neighborhood for the first time, I was immediately struck with the way everyone seemed to be related. All the men there are "brothers" and the women "sisters." I learned that using family language is a basic way of relating. "Aunts" and "uncles" are not necessarily related by birth. As often as not, they are caring neighbors or family friends. Children, I found, grow up with lots of "aunts" and "uncles," and most of them have godparents. Older people are expected to be grandparents to the neighborhood. Elderly men are often called "Pops"—a term of endearment for a grandfather.

For all that's tragic about inner-city family life—single-parent households, absent fathers, untutored children—there is much that is good. This same sense of a large, inclusive, extended family came to define our church. "We are family" is an overused cliché claimed for ulterior motives by football teams and sales organizations. But we really were family in that poverty-stricken neighborhood—a family of faith. For many people in that area of town, the church was their only meaningful family. I also quickly warmed to the fellowship when greeted by "Good to see you, brother."

It was there I came to realize that I have two families—a birth family and a belief family. Experiencing the rich African-American heritage of an extended family helped me appreciate God's extended family. My birth family, however good, is defined by biological boundaries. By contrast, there are no limits to God's family—everyone is a child of God. In that inner-city neighborhood I came to understand in a profound way that all people are God's children and therefore interconnected. And my birth family became even more meaningful as a metaphor of the world—a family without boundaries.

Tom Nees

4

Traits of a Healthy Home

*When we suffer from nostalgia, we fall
into the danger of selective memory. All of
the families of the past were not good families,
and all of the families of the present are
not hurting families.*

—Dolores Curran

MUCH OF WHAT WE HEAR ABOUT FAMILIES THESE DAYS SEEMS to be negative. From ministers to the media, the focus is often on what is wrong with modern families. Skyrocketing divorce rates, cohabitation, crack babies, abuse, adultery, teen violence, pregnancy out of wedlock—it's enough to make one ask: Is there any good news about families today?

The answer is yes. Sometimes we become so consumed with probing the problems, ferreting out weaknesses, and pointing out what's wrong that we don't even see what's right. This chapter takes a hard look at what's right with families. It looks at what takes place in a happy home and reveals the hallmarks of a healthy family.

Let me begin right from the top by saying that I am not

talking about the "perfect" family. I have never met one in my work. I didn't grow up in one. I don't live in one. And I suspect that such a family does not exist, except in fantasy. Real-life families have failures and foibles, but as this chapter will show, there is a discernible difference between families who are healthy versus those who are merely passable.

What Is a Healthy Family?

When John W. Hinckley Jr. attempted to assassinate United States President Ronald Reagan in 1981, commentators announced in a tone of wonder and mystification that little was known about Hinckley except that "he comes from a good family." What did they mean by "a good family"? That he had two parents at home, that they were religious, that they were respected in the community? The truth is that families aren't good simply because they have traditional signs of success. On the outside, a family can be filled with high achievers, live in a nice neighborhood, attend church regularly, and still be miserable on the inside. So what makes the difference?

Award-winning author Maggie Scarf spent eight years attempting to answer this question, and the result was her extraordinary book *Intimate Worlds*.[1] She outlines the structural blueprints that characterize most families' patterns of being and relating. On the low end of the continuum of family functioning are "severely disturbed" families. Then moving upward, one encounters the "polarized" and "rule-bound" families. And at the top of the scale are families belonging to the "optimal" group. As will become evident, families operating at these different levels are not only struggling with profoundly different kinds of dilemmas but also are struggling to deal with these dilemmas in very different ways. A brief overview, from worse to better, follows.

Level One: The Severely Disturbed Family

Scarf compares this family to a nation in a state of civil disorder, where nobody seems to have authority, and real leadership is totally lacking. It is a family in a state of confusion, turmoil, and pain. Little is predictable, and there are no clear-cut ways of behaving, because if any rules do exist, they are always changing. When a family member attempts to express an idea, another one will almost automatically dispute it. A sense of murky uncertainty pervades the entire family, and there are innumerable unresolved issues resulting in a family cauldron of sorrows and miseries. What this chaotic family is lacking, in the most fundamental way, is coherence.

Level Two: The Polarized Family

Though matters have improved relative to the disturbed family, things are still quite impaired for the polarized family. For in an effort to master the chaos and disorder, they have gone to the opposite extreme. Instead of having no rules, they have nothing but inflexible rules designed to control everything, including family members' actions, thoughts, and feelings. Everything becomes either/or, black or white. Scarf compares this family to a strong dictatorship in a country whose cultural institutions are breaking down, whose criminal justice system has ceased to function, and whose economy is out of control. Seen from this perspective, the emergence of a tyrannical parent feels adaptive, at least for a time, even though the family is bound by ironclad ways of doing everything, a kind of martial law. The polarized family is run, not by means of conflict resolution and compromise, but by means of intimidation and control.

Level Three: The Rule-Bound Family

After resolving the chaos and control of the previous levels, this family represents yet another advance upward. They have figured out how to maintain order and control in a less primitive fashion. In these families, control is no longer imposed upon its members by an oppressive dictator, but rather from within each individual family member. Their motto is "If you loved me, you would always do all the things that you know will meet with my approval." In other words, feeling worthy and loved is contingent on obeying the dictates of the family. The problem with this system is that when obedience to the rules takes precedence over any effort to figure out what one actually wants, it is almost impossible to make contact with one's own thoughts, wishes, and desires. The focus becomes "What *should* I be feeling?" instead of "What *am* I feeling?" And when this occurs, it is truly impossible to ever get to true intimacy. In the rule-bound family, members behave as they *ought to,* and as a result, real feelings are neither experienced nor expressed.

Level Four: The Optimal Family

Families at this healthier end of the continuum have achieved an ability to be comfortable with both their loving feelings and with their feelings of annoyance and frustration. In other words, family members take personal responsibility for their mixed, ambivalent thoughts and emotions and are willing to work them through. Families in this position generally find no conflict that cannot be resolved. According to Scarf, because their fundamental relationships with one another feel so secure, there is always the sense that "We can work it out." All feelings are taken to be the "facts" of someone's existence at that particular moment, because these families believe that the relationships they enjoy will not be threatened by one's real feelings. So even if one's feelings are critical or negative, the family members can be genuine with one another and thus build genuine understanding, affection, and intimacy.

The Qualities That Matter Most

As the previous levels of family functioning reveal, there are drastic differences between the patterns of dysfunctional families and healthy families. By taking a closer look at healthy families, we can more clearly prescribe changes from which every family can benefit.

I know of no author who has done a better job of defining these traits than Dolores Curran.[2] She compiled a list of desirable family traits and then had 500 family experts from the fields of religion, education, health, and family counseling select the qualities they perceive as most evident of a healthy family. Out of her list of 56 possible traits, the experts consistently selected 15 notables in the following order.

The healthy family . . .

    1. Communicates and listens.

2. Affirms and supports one another.
3. Teaches respect for others.
4. Develops a sense of trust.
5. Has a sense of play and humor.
6. Exhibits a sense of shared responsibility.
7. Teaches a sense of right and wrong.
8. Has a strong sense of family in which rituals and traditions abound.
9. Has a balance of interaction among members.
10. Has a shared religious core.
11. Respects the privacy of one another.
12. Values service to others.
13. Fosters family table time and conversation.
14. Shares leisure time.
15. Admits to and seeks help with problems.

While Curran admits that no family possesses all of these traits, thousands of happy families incorporate several of them into their ways of being (she believes a good start is just three or four). And these are the positive, healthy families who are not striving for perfection but are enjoyin., family life and the meaning it brings to their lives. Remember—they are not free from failure, conflict, or frustration; in fact, they expect difficult times as a part of family life. These families are free from the dysfunction, polarization, and rule-boundness that characterize families who are only hoping for a glimpse of these traits.

Questions for Reflection

- On the continuum describing the various levels of family functioning in this chapter, how would you view your own family?
- Do you know any examples of "optimal" families? If so, what is it that makes them so healthy?
- Why do you think communication and listening skills top the list of what makes a family healthy? How could it impact many of the other healthy traits?
- Why is it that unhealthy families too often equate "health" with "perfection"?

Try This Formula

Make a list of the things you like about your mate.

When I do that, the engineer's annoying habits somehow become transformed into more positive qualities. True, his toolboxes sometimes get in my way, but the power mower in the garage cost $5.00 and didn't work when my engineer bought it; now it could mow Iowa.

With minimal tinkering and trips to the hardware and electronics stores, he's also repaired a coffeepot, two hair dryers, the washing machine, a crooked floor lamp, assorted television sets, and the window, horn, and dome light on my car. One day I came home from the supermarket to find that he'd wired the living room, den, and basement for stereo. I figure that with all the money we've saved, I can feel free to stock up on another 20 pairs of shoes (a calculation that will undoubtedly bring him less joy than it does me).

As I think about it, the list grows longer. He listens when I give advice, he's good with the kids, he encourages me in new interests, he welcomes visits from my parents and other relatives, he gives me first chance at the Sunday crossword puzzle—well, you get the idea.[1]

Leola Floren

5

The Secret of a
Rock-Solid Marriage

Love does not consist of gazing at each other,
but in looking together in the same direction.
—*Antoine De Saint-Exupéry*

OUR FAMILY RECENTLY GATHERED AROUND A LARGE, CIRCULAR table in a restaurant that has unofficially become the backdrop for many of our most meaningful family celebrations. For decades our family has gathered here from around the country to mark holidays, birthdays, graduations, promotions, and farewells. But this time was different. The dinner was a celebration of Mom and Dad's 50th wedding anniversary. They didn't want a big party. This celebration was strictly a family affair.

The food was wonderful. The anniversary cake was lovely. The presents were nice, but not worthy of such a noble occasion. What impressed me most about the entire event, however, wasn't tangible. It was something my father said. We had just offered grace and thanked God for the family and the many years Mom and Dad had lived together. Then, before picking up his fork, he looked around the table and said, *"I can't believe it has been 50 years! The time is so short!"*

The rest of the meal was devoted to reminiscing. Mom talked

about the times when each of her three sons was born. She could describe in detail the various homes in which we lived. Dad talked about the churches and colleges he and Mom had served. There was the first pastorate they took during the Korean War and the transition to being a college president during the Middle East oil crisis. They both reminisced about their first trip to London and many other journeys around the globe. They must certainly have had some hard times, like all married couples do, but all they seemed to remember were things they enjoyed together.

I've thought a lot about my comparably short marriage of a dozen years since Mom and Dad celebrated their 50th anniversary. What will Leslie and I reminisce about after that many years? Have you ever thought about that? After 50 years, what memorable treasures will your house of love include?

Nothing is more important to the health and stability of your family than the state of your marriage. Family therapist Virginia Satir wrote that "the marital relationship is the axis around which all other family relationships are formed. The mates are the 'architects' of the family." For this reason, I devote this chapter to building a rock-solid marriage. As a psychologist who speaks to thousands of couples and counsels dozens more each year, I pay special attention to couples who have built a long-lasting and deeply satisfying marriage. And after years of study, I have uncovered a fundamental secret: *Who you are in your marriage is more important than what you do.* Marital skills such as communication and conflict resolution are critically important to building a strong marriage; but happy couples know that before these skills can take root, one must first focus on who he or she is as a marriage partner. So in the remainder of this chapter I pose a number of questions, not about what you are doing, but about *who you are being.*

Are You a Safe Person?

A close relationship is built on feelings of security. As any beginning psychology student knows, safety is a fundamental human need—more important than love or self-worth. If we do not feel safe, little else is of much consequence. The same holds true in marriage. For example, if your partner doesn't feel safe with you, if he or she fears rejection, there is little hope of him or her ever opening up, sharing inner thoughts and feelings, and being authentic. To create a sense of security for the one you love, you must, of course, keep your word. Each broken promise, no matter how small, becomes an insect eating away at your foundation of safety. Each confidence that is broken chips away at it too. For this reason, successful couples take great care to protect one another's secrets and to follow through on their commitments.

Are You a Forgiving Person?

In *Love in the Time of Cholera,* Nobel laureate Gabriel García Márquez portrays a marriage that disintegrates over a bar of soap. It was the wife's job to keep the house in order, including the soap in the bathroom. One day she forgot to replace the soap. Her husband exaggerated the oversight: "I've been bathing for almost a week without any soap." She vigorously denied forgetting to replace the soap. Although she had indeed forgotten, her pride was at stake, and she would not back down. For the next seven months they slept in separate rooms and ate in silence. "Even when they were old and placid," writes Márquez, "they were very careful about bringing it up, for the barely healed wounds could begin to bleed again as if they had been inflicted only yesterday."

How could a bar of soap ruin a marriage? The answer is actually simple: Because neither partner would say, "Forgive me." Forgiveness is the only way to break the inevitable cycle of blame and pain that every marriage encounters.

Are You Someone Who Listens?

At the heart of every good relationship is the ability to listen and understand what the other person is saying. Without accurate listening, a rock-solid marriage could never be built. While this is a quality that can be refined through learning some skills, listening begins with a genuine desire to understand your partner. So be the kind of person who takes the time to hear what it is that your partner is saying. Don't make it a habit to interrupt or jump to conclusions in your communication. Instead, patiently allow your partner to say what is on his or her mind.

Next, listen to the feelings expressed, and let the other person know you hear what he or she is saying. As a mirror reflects an image, you can reflect your partner's message by saying something like, "What I hear you saying is . . ." This kind of a reflection lets your partner know you are really interested in accurately understanding.

Are You Someone Who Can Receive?

When the scales of a relationship are unbalanced—when one is always receiving and the other is always giving—both people will eventually feel cheated. In healthy relationships, however, people meet each other's needs. There is a give-and-take that keeps both people in balance. Are you the kind of person who gives but finds it difficult to receive? If so, allow your partner to care for you as much as you care for him or her. Don't fall into the trap of thinking that to be a good spouse, you have to do *all* the giving. While it may be "more blessed to give than to receive" (Acts 20:35), sometimes in marriage receiving from your partner is one of the greatest gifts you can offer.

Are You a Person of Promise?

Author Fred Smith tells the story of an experience he had in a doughnut shop in Grand Saline, Texas. A young farm couple was sitting at the table next to his. The man was wearing overalls, and the woman had on a gingham dress. After finishing their doughnuts, the man got up to pay the bill, but his wife didn't get up to follow him. After paying the check, her husband came back and stood in front of her. She put her arms around his neck, and he lifted her up, revealing that she was wearing a full-body brace. He lifted her out of her chair and backed out the front door to the pickup truck, with her hanging from his neck. As the man gently put his wife into the truck, everyone in the shop watched. No one said anything until a waitress remarked, almost reverently, "He took his vows seriously."

How about you? Do you think about your wedding vows and the promise you made to your spouse? If so, you know the strength that comes from being a committed life partner.

Do You Walk in Your Partner's Shoes?

"I can't believe you didn't buy the cereal I like."

"Wait a minute—you share responsibility for groceries, too, you know."

"Don't try to pass the blame to me—you said you'd buy it."

"Yes, but I told you to remind me."

"Why should I? It's your responsibility."

Such inane conversation bleats on and on in marriage until one of the partners takes the time to empathize. Once either one of them sees things from the other's perspective, everything changes. Suddenly they understand how a simple mistake could occur ("She's had a lot on her mind with the stress at work") and how an unmet expectation can lead to frustration ("He was really counting on his midnight snack as a reward for finishing his project"). Empathy eases the tension in marriage, because it reveals why a person might react, feel, and think the way he or she does. Of course, empathy does not come naturally—it takes work. It takes a decision to see life as another person sees it. But the spouses who focus on being an empathetic partner enjoy the relational dividends that only empathy can bring.

Are You Willing to Weather Turbulence?

Almost every good relationship eventually encounters a rough spot, a time when both partners feel like giving up. It is a scary phase in relationships, usually indicating that we are going beneath the surface to talk about our true feelings, the good and the bad. It's a time of griping and whining, complaining and accusing. But if we are mature enough, and if we persevere, the time of relational turbulence can lead to a deeper, more genuine, and more authentic relationship than before. Conflict, in fact, is often the price we pay for a deepening intimacy in marriage.

Are You a Person of God?

While I was listening to Mom and Dad reminisce at their 50th wedding anniversary, something else struck me—their utter dependence on God. It is impossible to separate their spiritual formation from their marital maturity. They are living proof to me that no single factor does more to cultivate oneness and a meaningful sense of purpose in marriage than a shared commitment to spiritual discovery. Sharing life's ultimate meaning with another person is the call of soul mates. Spirituality is to your marriage as yeast is to a loaf of bread. We have said to hundreds of couples: Ultimately, your spiritual commitment will determine whether your marriage rises successfully or falls disappointingly flat.

Before I close this chapter, I want to make one point clear: The idea that a marriage "just works" or "just doesn't work" is simply not true. We know too much about what it takes to build a successful marriage these days to allow this false belief to go unquestioned. The truth is that any two people who are willing to work at being good marriage partners can build a rock-solid marriage. So no matter what condition your marriage is in today, whether you are struggling to hold on or flying high, answering the preceding questions in the affirmative will help you build a fulfilling marriage that will go the distance.

Will you look back while celebrating 50 years of marriage and say, "I can't believe time is so short"? I pray you will. For, "As a bridegroom rejoices over his bride, so will your God rejoice over you" (Isaiah 62:5).

Questions for Reflection
- Do you agree with the point that the health of a family

is determined by the state of a couple's marriage? Why or why not?

- One of the important qualities of a successful marriage is taking one's vows seriously. How might you do this in a concrete and practical way?
- What do you make of the observation that who you are in marriage is more important than what you do? Why do you think this is so?
- How can couples cultivate spiritual intimacy in their marriages? Have you discovered any personal strategies with your own partner?

Family Worship

Of particular interest was [John] Wesley's insightful plan for family worship. In order to help parents who had little or no experience with such things, he set a precise order for family worship. The family was gathered, and a short prayer opened the session. This was followed by psalm singing. Next came Bible study. The passage was read aloud by a parent. Following the reading, one parent explained the passage. Then the children were to explain the passage back to the parents in their own words. This method is ingenious educationally. It requires the parents to study the passage thoroughly enough to explain it so a child can understand. Further, it provides opportunity to check the child's grasp of the lesson when the child attempts to reexplain the passage.

After the Bible study came prayer. It started with a written prayer from A Collection of Prayers for Families. This was to be followed by appropriate extemporary prayer, which included prayer for each family member. Then came the singing of the doxology, and the pronouncement of a benediction by a parent, usually the father.

This was followed by one of the most important parts of this spiritual formation practice. Each child was to ask for a blessing. In response, father or mother laid hands on the child's head and blessed the child in Jesus' name. Wesley warned parents that no matter how unpleasant or disobedient the child had been that day, under no circumstances was this blessing to be denied.[1]

Imagine what it would mean to a child to be blessed in the name of Jesus by his or her parents every day. Would it not do more for the generation gap than even the sagacious counsel of Dr. Spock?[2]

Wesley D. Tracy

6

Raising Kids Right

by Les Parrott Sr.

*Traditions give balance to our lives,
or else we would be like a fiddler on the roof.*
—*Tevye in* Fiddler on the Roof

TRADITION! TRADITION! UNLESS WE HAVE GOOD FAMILY TRADI-
tions, we are like a fiddler on the roof, playing a merry tune
but with scant defense against a slippery slope.

More than 30 years ago the award-winning musical *Fiddler on the Roof* caught the attention of many people during a
decade when long-standing family traditions were being
downsized, even discarded. The traditional institutions of
family, home, church, school, and even law were being re-
placed by fiddlers playing new tunes on the housetops. Their
unfamiliar songs were about rights (even children's rights),
new sexual freedoms, the demise of institutional religion, and
the death of the family as we had known it.

Americans contemplated the role of Tevye, a poor Jewish
milkman with five unmarried daughters to support in the village of Anatevka in czarist Russia. With a sharp-tongued wife
at home and growing anti-Semitism in the village, Tevye talks
to God about his troubles as though they were on personal

terms. Traditions keep him strong when his existence is as precarious as a fiddler on the roof.

It was during this era, when Americans were humming tunes like "Sunrise, Sunset," "If I Were a Rich Man," or "Matchmaker, Matchmaker," that we were in the process of raising boys at our house.

At this time I was living with my best friend and closest confidante. I still am! That relationship, which included the ability to talk about things for long periods of time, was one of our strengths in trying to raise our sons. I don't remember that we ever read Dr. Spock. We never attended any seminars on parenting or, for that matter, read any books on the subject.

But we had a place to walk and talk that could not be beat. We would walk along the seashore. As we walked and talked, and walked some more, and talked some more, the boys built sand castles or played games. We packed our station wagon— the answer to family transportation before there were vans— picked up the boys at school on Friday afternoon, and headed for Cannon Beach, Oregon, returning Saturday after lunch.

It was during these walks that Lora Lee—best friend, confidante, and wife—and I discussed, sorted out, and decided on the results we would work for in raising our three sons. There were two ideals we decided to strive for: First, we wanted our boys to understand, accept, and internalize our faith and values. And second, we wanted each of them to have an adequate education for life and for the careers they proposed to follow.

We expected each of the boys to personalize his faith and values. We did not want them to reject out of hand what we believed, the church we loved, and the personal values we espoused because we allowed ourselves to become alienated from them. I had seen too often what happened in homes where communication was wrapped in anger.

I particularly did not want the boys to turn against our most cherished beliefs as a way of striking back at me as their father. I traveled frequently during this era. My time away could have given the boys reason to believe I didn't care about them when my schedule conflicted with their games and other events. The bulk of parenting was left to their mother, which could have put them at even greater distance from me. These were givens in the dynamics of our family that would need to be worked out in future "talking walks" on the beach.

Passing the Faith On from One Generation to Another

Passing on faith and family ethics is not an exact science. We were fortunate to have the help of an outstanding youth pastor and the support of a loving congregation. Although all three of our boys are now ordained ministers with strong marriages and a commitment to Christian ethics, I am not sure we did things right or would do them the same way again if we were starting over.

But for good or ill, here are some of the things we decided to do at our house. These were strategies about how to raise kids right, strategies we developed during those long talks:

1. Our kids would never hear us criticize a member of the church board.

We determined that none of the boys would ever hear us say anything critical about any member of the church and especially the church board. We even found excuses to hold board meetings and committee sessions in the parsonage so the boys could get to know the church leaders. At an appropriate time in each of these home gatherings, refreshments were served by the boys from a small red wagon that they pulled around the room. When they were older, one of the boys presented the matter of a basketball hoop to the board, and they voted in his favor.

2. Our kids would learn to respect and appreciate clergy leaders.

We served meals to church dignitaries with the boys at the table. It was during one of these meals that a leader asked one of the boys—by this time in high school—what he expected to be when he finished college. He replied without hesitation—and I nearly swallowed a chicken bone—that he planned to be an outstanding fund-raiser. We had never talked about this, and he had never mentioned it to his mother or me. But today he is a college president.

Another time when we had a church leader at our table, I told our guest in advance that we would be having hamburgers and baked beans because Lora Lee didn't want the boys to think church leaders were so special they could not enjoy the same kinds of food we had on ordinary days.

There is no need for me to give more anecdotal evidence of the things we did to build confidence in our boys as they watched clergy leadership.

3. The kids would have an underpinning of Bible knowledge.

I became convinced that our boys needed to know and understand the Bible from beginning to end. We also came to believe that all Christian faith begins with an underpinning of knowledge concerning the narrative of the Old and New Testaments.

My mother taught me the Bible narrative by daily mid-morning readings from a Bible story book, beginning when I was four or five years old. If I could not tell the story back to her when she finished reading it, she read it again. Or we acted it out. I well remember when we acted out the story of Jonah—she was the storm.

We developed a study program that included 200 Bible stories, major chapters, and the most basic theology for children. Along with our Sunday School, children's church, and Wednesday evening children's meetings, programs, and lots of repetition and review, our boys learned the Bible.

It was during a narrative study of the Crucifixion that one of our boys was led to the Lord by his mother in the kitchen after she had let him smell the vinegar like what they had given Jesus. She seized the moment when he started to cry.

A Closing Word

The final chapter has not been written. Our boys are in their 30s and 40s now, and there is plenty of time for the fiddlers on the roof to do their thing. But one thing is certain: Their mother and I took seriously the matter of choosing preferred outcomes in raising our sons. We persistently gave ourselves to these strategies—either good or bad for this later time— that we prayerfully believed would bring the outcomes to pass.

Your outcomes and strategies for your children will need to be developed against a whole new set of fiddlers who seem determined to sidetrack the most worthwhile traditions in our lives. But generational faith and continuing family values are not beyond our reach if we care enough to identify the values and then do something to perpetuate them in the lives of our children.

Questions for Reflection

- What "fiddlers" in your life tend to distract your purposes more than others?
- What preferred results would you like to see in the raising of your own children?
- What traditions in your family are held in highest esteem?
- On a scale of 1 to 10, how important in your mind is education for your children?
- What are some personal policies you follow in helping your children increase their faith through their experiences with the church and its people?
- Even if you feel the kids have not been raised right, is it too late, or do you have things that could be done to help them?

Divorce and Children

Divorce is a wrenching experience for many adults and almost all children. It is nearly always more devastating for children than for their parents.[1]

If I had the power to eliminate the evils that impact children's lives, I would begin by doing away with divorce. This is a strong statement in a world in which thousands of children suffer physical, emotional, and sexual abuse. I don't underestimate the horrors of those evils. However, I believe divorce is more devastating for two reasons.

First, it affects such an overwhelming number of boys and girls. According to George Barna, two out of three children born around 1993 will eventually live in a single-parent household.[2] More than half of today's baby busters have experienced divorce personally, and four-fifths have had friends who experienced divorce.[3]

Second, divorce touches nearly every aspect of a child's life, and many of the changes are permanent. Family relationships, economic situation, self-esteem, security, optimism, worldview—these are only a few conditions that divorce changes, often forever. Children of divorce deal with feelings of guilt, rejection, and loss. They often receive less care than children from intact families. Many must adopt an adult's role long before they are ready to do so. Divorce is not an issue that children can deal with once and for all and then forget. For many, problems created by divorce recur periodically throughout their lives.[4]

When I look ahead and think about a world filled with adults who grew up "divorced," I worry. One young man compared divorce with murder and concluded that divorce is worse because its "lifelong damaging effects . . . at the deepest level."[5] If this is so, what kind of world do people like this young man create or perpetuate?

It would be easy to be overwhelmed with pessimism when thinking about such questions. Thankfully, I believe in a God who works redemptively, amid "worst possible" scenarios. I challenge the Church to work in partnership with God to prevent divorce when possible and to reclaim and revitalize the lives of children of divorce.

Miriam J. Hall

7

When Families
Self-destruct

*Nobody's family can hang out the sign
Nothing the Matter Here.*

—*Chinese proverb*

FOR THE FIRST TIME IN HISTORY, A PERSON MARRYING NOW IS more likely to lose a spouse through divorce than through death. Each year 1.2 million children see their parents split up. Like high school graduation or getting a driver's license, divorce has almost become a rite of passage for children. If current rates of divorce continue, 40 percent will become children of divorce by the age of 18.

For most of our history we have had stringent guidelines and procedures preventing divorce. Divorce happened, but it was rare. In fact, the divorce rate crept steadily upward very gradually, so slowly that we barely noticed. But in the early 1970s something dramatic happened. Before that time, divorce in nearly all instances was universally acknowledged as a horrible event. Divorce proceedings were ugly, detailed airings of connubial crimes as husband and wife squared off in court to fight over money, children, and one another's morals. But then California instituted the no-fault divorce, and almost instantly it was accepted nationwide. With this act, power was shifted overwhelmingly from the spouse who wanted to stay married to the spouse who wanted to call it quits. The court system thus became a mere rubber-stamp reviewer of agreements hammered out between spouses and their lawyers.

The advent of no-fault divorce was hailed as a quick and easy solution to relationships gone sour. But now, a generation later, many divorced parents and their children are emerging to paint a far different picture: one of financial travail, psychological devastation, and endless emotional turmoil. Divorce is particularly harmful to women and children. No-fault reforms have robbed women of alimony, and no-fault's lax child-support enforcement has allowed men to default on their obligations to the point at which many divorced women and children are reduced to poverty. The emotional fallout of divorce is easy to see. Numerous divorced people, their attorneys, their therapists, their children, and their children's therapists have learned that divorce is shattering.

Perhaps it should come as no surprise that divorce is so common. Relatively little attention is given to helping couples learn the rudiments of marriage and family; a marriage license is easier to obtain than a driver's license. Once a couple realizes they have developed some unhealthful or destructive patterns, they typically become too lost in their anger to seek help. Where once they might have recognized that they had workable emotional problems, now one or the other is simply convinced that he or she is no longer in love. In *Christianity Today,* Virginia Stern Owens has written, "It seems we know how to do almost everything else in this country except how to make lasting marriages and raise children."

Uncoupling

Whatever the reasons for divorce, the stages of the separation are fairly predictable. Sociologist Diane Vaughan calls this process "uncoupling." The process begins as a quiet, unilateral process. Usually one person, the initiator, is unhappy or dissatisfied but keeps such feelings to himself or herself. The initiator often ponders fundamental questions about his or her identity: "Who am I? Who am I in this relationship?" The dissatisfied partner may attempt to make changes in the relationship, but these are often unsuccessful, as he or she may not really know what the problem is.

Because the dissatisfied partner is unable to find satisfaction within the relationship, he or she begins turning elsewhere. This is not a malicious or intentional turning away; it is done to find self-validation without leaving the relationship. However, in doing so, Vaughan says, the dissatisfied partner "creates a small territory independent of the coupled identity." This creates a division within the relationship. Gradually the dissatisfied partner voices more and more complaints, which make the relationship and partner increasingly undesirable. The initiator begins thinking about alternatives to the relationship and comparing the costs and benefits of these alternatives. Meanwhile, both the initiator and his or her partner try to cover up the seriousness of the dissatisfaction, submerging it in the little problems of everyday living.

Eventually the initiator decides that he or she can no longer go on and tells the partner that the relationship is over, or he or she breaks a fundamental rule in the relationship, such as by having an extramarital affair.

Uncoupling does not end when the end of a relationship is announced, or even when the couple physically separate. Acknowledging that the relationship cannot be saved represents the beginning of the last stage of uncoupling. "Getting over a relationship," Vaughan writes, "does not mean relinquishing that part of our life that we shared with another, but rather coming to some conclusion that allows us to accept and understand its altered significance."[1]

Although separation generally precedes divorce, not all separations lead to divorce. As many as one couple out of every six that remains married is likely to have separated for at least two days.[2] One study found that of those who separated, 40 percent reconciled at least once.[3] So if you are separated and teetering on the edge of divorce, I urge you to give it time. Perhaps you want emotional distance, or maybe you need to allow your anger to dissipate. That's understandable. But don't give up on marriage if you find yourself being pulled in that direction. By all means, seek out a competent marriage counselor who can give you and your partner objective help.

If you have already suffered a divorce and children were involved, great care must be taken to ensure as much comfort for them as possible. The following dos and don'ts can help.

Dos and Don'ts with Your Children After Divorce

According to 1988 data from the National Center for Health Statistics, children from divorced families are two to three times as likely to suffer emotional and behavioral problems as those from intact families. And parents reeling under their own emotional or financial problems are often the last to notice. When their children become aggressive, withdrawn, angry, depressed, or begin to have difficulties with friends or schoolwork, parents may overlook the problems as normal or expected under the circumstances. Few divorced parents realize that some children suffer lasting scars even if outward signs of stress dissipate as they get older.

Two major factors, if they are present, seem to protect children when their parents divorce. These are having parents who are psychologically and morally healthy and who are sensitive and committed to the children.[4] In the absence of a parent who can fill this bill, grandparents or other family members, or even a mentor like a teacher or adult friend, can sometimes be very helpful. The bottom line is that divorce weakens the child rearing and protective functions of the family. Here are a few suggestions from the experts on how to keep these fundamental family functions strong even when the bow breaks.

Reassure, reassure, reassure. Your children need to hear from you over and over again that they were not responsible for the breakup, and that nothing they did or said made it happen. This reassurance is not easily absorbed by most kids, especially by young children, so be intentional about getting this message through. In the context of this reassurance you can own the responsibility by apologizing for hurting them and causing such disruption in their lives. Also, invite their feedback and suggestions, and take them seriously.

Make up carefully for past mistakes. "Everything I do in my life is for my children," confessed one divorced mom with three children. Indulgence taken too far—either giving children too much leeway or showering them with material goods—does not convey love, and it does not make up for loss. When you are overindulging your children, you are doing it for you, to ease your conscience, not for your children. Some professionals call the problem "marshmallowing," in which a parent does anything and everything for the child, attempting to cushion any possible fall. This kind of overprotection and overinvolvement always backfires.

Stay fully present. There is a flip side to the overindulging phenomenon that occurs when the parent finds it impossible to give to his or her children what he or she didn't get as a child, notably the love and attention of the noncustodial parent. Following the breakup of a marriage, almost 90 percent of children continue to make their home with their mother. As time goes by, studies have shown, many see less and less of their fathers, and some lose contact entirely. Do your children a favor by not letting this happen.

Don't "parentalize" your children. Sondra, age 39, was 6 when her parents split up and 8 when they remarried (within days of each other); their new spouses also had children. She says, "My parents constantly used me as a messenger: 'Tell your father not to send his check late,' or 'Tell your mother that I want you to be with our family at Christmas.' At either end, I knew that the messages would not be well received. There was a lot of pressure on me to worry about the logistics of the family, to be the peacemaker, to be old before my time." Making a child take on responsibilities that are inappropriate for a child is terribly destructive.

Whatever the custody arrangements, divorce often robs children of both parents. Parenting abilities cannot help but be interfered with during a divorce, so kids end up trying to cope not only with the split but also with the fact that they've lost both parents' emotional availability. The following suggestions, however, can help make this difficult process a bit less difficult for children.

If Your Parents Got Divorced

Studies have found that divorce rates are higher for people who grew up with divorced parents than for those raised in intact households. One reason for this is that the unresolved issues they have with parents contaminate their own marriages. Even as adults, children of divorce are eager to create a successful family; for example, they are often struggling to let their spouse in as full partner in that process. Trust and the sharing of feelings and emotions can be threatening, so children of divorce hold back.

Yet a child of divorce need not be condemned to repeating the past. Consider the following suggestions for how to move forward. Coming to terms with the impact of divorce is not an easy task to accomplish on one's own, though; you may want to explore any or all of these issues with a trusted counselor.

1. *Acknowledge, examine, and try to resolve the anger you still feel over your parents' divorce and its aftermath.* There are many good reasons for doing this, not the least of which is the potential that anger has to destroy other relationships.

2. *Learn how to manage conflict.* If you were taught to handle disagreements by walking away from them, learn to communicate what is bothering you. On the other hand, if the behavior you grew up with was confrontational (if there was yelling or abuse), strive to change the pattern, for example, by setting a specific time with your partner, or your children, when troubling matters can be raised, discussed, and resolved.

3. *Strive to gain self-confidence.* Many children of divorce carry into adulthood the feeling "If I had been better, my parents would have stayed together." This lack of self-esteem affects all future relationships, including those with your part-

ner and your child. Understanding that you did not cause the divorce, that a parent leaves a marriage because of unhappiness with a spouse, not with a child, can free you to create your own family, unfettered by the pull of the past.

4. *Ask your parents to explain, adult to adult now, why the divorce took place.* Don't lecture. Don't judge. Don't personalize. Try to understand the situation they were in and the pressures they grew up with in their own families of origin. Understanding your parents is an important step toward letting go of the pain of the past and moving with greater confidence toward the future.

Keep Moving Forward

The past does not have to dictate the present. Studies affirm the therapeutic benefits—for those who grew up with divorce—of committing to marriage and building families of their own. Becoming a parent gives the child of divorce a second chance at a family. It is an opportunity to succeed and to heal.

So don't give in to the temptation of believing you have inherited a genetic marital flaw or that you are somehow defective. As Prov. 4:18 says, "The path of the righteous is like the first gleam of dawn, shining ever brighter till the full light of day."

Questions for Reflection

- How do you explain the sharp rise in the divorce rate in recent decades? Besides the no-fault legislation, what can help explain it?
- It is difficult to find anyone whose life has not been deeply affected by divorce. How has a family breakup close to you affected you?
- Consider how a family breakup impacts children. What do you believe is the most destructive aspect of divorce for children?
- Scripture says that hope is the anchor of our soul (Heb. 6:19). What hope can you offer someone who is considering divorce?

Personal Time with God

As important as sharing devotions is in spiritual bonding, this is not a substitute for a private quiet time with God. Your own time to learn to relate intimately with the Heavenly Father is vital to your spiritual growth.

There is, however, at least one warning we should heed—it is possible to become a spiritual "snob"! In fact, you probably know people who are exactly that. They are the ones whose talk is full of special messages direct from God. They manage just to let it slip that they have spent so many minutes in prayer and that they have certainly remembered you and your last trial with your spouse. You worry a bit at such a statement and whether this individual has shared the confidence with another person as well as with God.

Now this may seem at first a bit cynical, but it isn't. The most deeply spiritual people with the greatest devotional lives are usually fairly quiet about it. They live out God's love and power in a quietly humble way that speaks more loudly than sermons. A saint of old has admonished succinctly, "Preach Christ! And if you must, use words!"

You can readily see that if your spiritual life and growth outstrip your spouse's, a barrier will develop, rather than a bond. If you suspect such a thing is happening, seek special guidance from the Lord. God will guide you so that your spiritual life will not be stunted, and also so that you will not grow away from each other.

Always be alert for any destructive degree of competition. Healthy rivalry spurs you on in the growth process. That which is not healthy puts down and denigrates the other; this must be avoided at all costs.

Throughout life there is a constant search for proper balance. Being open and honest with each other is vital to a healthy marriage. But the balance for openness is the ability to have periods of comfortable silence. In achieving personal spiritual maturity, without putting down your mate, you may well need the skill of studied quietness.[1]

Grace Ketterman

8

Saving a Marriage Before It Starts

We have been poisoned by fairy tales.

—Anais Nin

ED SULLIVAN INVITED INGRID BERGMAN TO APPEAR ON HIS POPU-lar television program around 1958, when she was living with an Italian film producer. Bergman left her husband and had a child. Before she actually went on the show, there was such a public clamor that Sullivan pulled the plug.

Can you imagine? Today every time Elizabeth Taylor gets married, it's a kind of national holiday for the media. The difference in the public reaction toward Ingrid Bergman then and Elizabeth Taylor now reveals a tragic trend of enormous consequence.

The "till death do us part" of the marriage vow rings increasingly ironic. We've all heard the startling statistics saying 50 percent or more of today's marriages will not survive. What we know for sure is that 200,000 new marriages each year end prior to the couples' second anniversaries.[1] The numbers can be interpreted and debated, but most marriage experts agree that divorce is epidemic and choking our society. For too many of today's new couples, marriage has become "till divorce do us part."

Equally startling as the predictions and statistics, however, is the fact that *fewer than a fifth of all marriages in America are preceded by some kind of formal marriage preparation.* And since three out of four United States marriages are blessed by a member of the clergy, columnist Michael McManus has come to call churches "blessing machines."[2] He makes a good point. The truth is that most engaged couples prepare more for their weddings than they do for their marriages. The millions upon millions of bridal magazines sold each year can testify to that. They are filled with information about wedding ceremonies and honeymoons—but rarely a sentence on marriage itself.

Seven Critical Questions

Working on the campus of a Christian university, my wife, Leslie, and I have seen numerous couples fall in love, get engaged, marry, and hope for the best. But we have also witnessed our fair share of wedding-bell blues, marital separation, and fractured families.

"By wisdom a house is built," says Proverbs, "and through *understanding* it is established; through *knowledge* its rooms are filled with rare and beautiful treasures" (24:3-4, emphasis added). Because a house is built on understanding and knowledge, couples should ask and answer some specific questions if they are to discover "beautiful treasures." Here are seven pertinent questions:

Question 1: *Have you faced the myths of marriage with honesty?*

Underlying many romantic relationships is a faulty foundation of marital myths. Dealing with this early on helps demythologize marriage and free couples from misguided assumptions. One of the most common and harmful myths couples believe is "We expect exactly the same things from marriage." Consciously and unconsciously, couples assume their lifelong partner has the same mental image of what marriage should and will be like. But it isn't so. Because of their individual backgrounds, couples bring diverse role expectations and many unconscious rules for living.

Two additional common myths are "Everything good in our relationship will get better, and everything bad will disappear." Of course, these don't hold water either. *Not* everything gets better. Couples inevitably go through a mourning process, grieving over what they lose by getting married (for example, giving up childhood). And marriage does not erase difficulty. Only Cinderella and other fictional characters live "happily ever after."

Perhaps the most unhealthful myth needing to be addressed in this session is "My spouse will make me whole." Proverbs says, "As iron sharpens iron, so one person sharpens another" (27:17). Marriage is a God-given way to improve and hone our beings, but marriage is not a substitute for personal growth. Couples who swallow this myth become overly dependent and enmeshed.

The bottom line of this session? It's simple. Liberated from these myths, couples can settle into the real world of marriage—with all its joys and sorrows, passions and pains.

Question 2: *Can you identify your love style?*

Most engaged couples analyze love in quantitative terms: "How much do we love each other?" Asked enough, this question will eventually lead couples to believe that Cupid's arrow has lost its punch and that they should call it quits. It is far more revealing for couples to examine love in qualitative terms: "In what ways do we express love?" This question focuses on what love is and how its style changes—sometimes logical, romantic, unselfish, possessive, and so on.

Yale psychologist Robert Sternberg uses a triangle to illustrate how love works:[3]

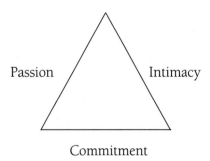

This simple triangle can be used to help couples see how the ingredients of love—passion, intimacy, and commitment—fluctuate from time to time and how one's love style may sometimes be out of sync with his or her partner. Newlyweds who equate true love only with passion, for example, are doomed to disappointment. By showing couples that these three ingredients can vary, they begin to see that love is fluid, and the three components of love can increase and decrease independently—but it doesn't mean one has "fallen out of love."

No couple newly in love wants to hear that their flame will burn lower in time; but we have to let them know their love will change shape, and their feelings will fade from time to time. The passionate love that begins a marriage cannot sustain a marriage. Teaching couples the fundamentals of love prepares them for inevitable changes in their love styles and helps them go the distance. As 19th-century preacher Henry Ward Beecher said, "Young love is a flame; very pretty, very hot and fierce, but still only light and flickering. The love of the older and disciplined heart is as coals, deep-burning, unquenchable."

Question 3: *Have you developed the habit of happiness?*

One of my favorite textbooks, considered a classic by many, contains this italicized sentence: *"The most important characteristic of a marriageable person is the habit of happiness."* Question 3 helps focus on the couple's capacity to adjust to things beyond their control and be happy anyhow. Too often this important quality is overlooked in marriage preparation, and couples end up believing that happiness is a matter of luck rather than will. Millions of couples, in fact, are robbed of happiness because one of the partners has developed a negative mind-set and sabotaged the marriage with blame, self-pity, or resentment. That's why we focus on the individuals of the couple and challenge them to master the art of adjusting to things beyond their control. This habit can be learned by observing and listening to an older couple who have survived a life jolt (for example, a job loss or major illness) to discover how they made it. This exercise is well worth the investment, and it just may be the key to cultivating a habit that can make or break a young marriage.

Question 4: *Can you say what you mean and understand what you hear?*

Perhaps the most commonplace problem couples face in marriage is a breakdown in communication. Whether a marriage sinks or swims depends on how well partners send and receive messages—how well they say what they mean and understand what they hear. And the best time to build communication skills is when things are going well—in the very earliest stages of marriage. The goal of this session is to help each person become more understanding and better understood.

Before focusing on a "list of dos and don'ts" for good communication, couples need to learn the bedrock skill of empathy. Once they learn to put themselves in each other's shoes, the guidelines for good communication fall more naturally into place. In Ephesians Paul writes, "Do not let any unwholesome talk come out of your mouths, but only what is helpful for building others up according to their needs" (4:29). Empathy allows couples to do just that—build one another up. Empathy also becomes the springboard for practicing James's admonition: "Be quick to listen, slow to speak" (1:19). With a solid foundation of empathy, couples are more likely to practice reflective listening and truly understand one another.

Question 5: *Have you bridged the gender gap?*

"There are three things that are too amazing for me, four that I do not understand: the way of an eagle in the sky, the way of a snake on a rock, the way of a ship on the high seas, and the way of a man with a maiden" (Prov. 30:18-19). The contrasts between women and men *are* sometimes striking! Question 5 helps couples realize, by virtue of being the opposite sex, how each partner thinks, feels, and behaves differently. If these differences are heeded and accounted for, they can become the source of greater intimacy in marriage. The key, of course, is not simply to recognize the differences, but to *appreciate* them too. By identifying their top 10 needs, couples can identify how their personal needs differ and propose ways of meeting those unique needs. This begins the important process of bridging the gender gap.

Question 6: *Do you know how to fight a good fight?*

It generally takes very little for the fur to fly in most marriages. But that's difficult to accept when your relationship is just blooming. Couples must learn that conflict is not necessarily bad, but the *way* couples argue can be.

The research of University of Washington psychologist John Gottman has revealed what to watch for when conflict erupts. In fact, after two decades of study, he has been able to predict at a 95 percent accuracy rate which marriages will survive and which will fail—based solely on *how* a couple fights. The four disastrous ways of interacting, in order of least to most dangerous, are criticism, contempt, defensiveness, and stonewalling.[4]

Couples can reduce their toxic quarrel quotient, but heeding these red flags is critically important for engaged and newly married couples. Steering clear of them is perhaps the best preventative medicine they can take against divorce. When couples learn to fight a good fight, they deepen their intimacy and understand what Augustine meant when he said, "Love can be angry . . . with a kind of anger in which there is no gall, like the dove's and not the raven's."

Question 7: *Are you and your partner soul mates?*

Perhaps the most important and least talked-about aspect of a healthy marriage is the spiritual dimension. A couple can demythologize marriage, understand love styles, develop the habit of happiness, communicate clearly, bridge the gender gap, and fight a good fight—and still long for a deeper connection. Why? There is in all of us, at the very center of our lives, a tension, a burning in the heart that is deep and insatiable. Our hearts are restless until they rest in God (Augustine's famous truism). Most couples expect marriage to quench their soulful longing, and it often does for a time. But for many, the deep, restless aching echoes again. It is extremely important that couples cultivate spiritual intimacy—finding God in their marriage. Couples need to know that marriage can reveal God's faithfulness and His forgiveness. They need to know how to tend the soul of their marriage. They need to know that worshiping together, prayer, and service, for example, can help them walk together with God.

Sharing life's ultimate meaning with another person is the call of soul mates. Spirituality is to marriage as yeast is to a loaf of bread. Ultimately a couple's spiritual commitment will determine whether their marriage rises successfully or falls disappointingly flat. Partners without a spiritual depth of oneness can never compete with the fullness of love that soul mates enjoy.

These seven questions can help new couples prepare for marriage. But once these questions have been explored, the real work of "saving a marriage before it begins" starts. And if you are in a healthy, mature marriage, you can do a great deal to help. That's where marriage mentoring comes in.

Marriage Mentors

A most significant component of marriage preparation involves linking a young couple with a more mature, experienced couple for a mentoring relationship. My wife and I have seen hundreds of couples strengthen their new marriages through the mentoring that comes from a healthy, objective couple who will walk with them and invest in them during their first year of marriage. The idea is simple: the couples meet at one month after the wedding, seven months, and at the one-year mark. Each meeting has a unique focus and offers newlyweds a place to get objective input from a couple who has "been there."

By the way, there is a boomerang effect to marriage mentoring. Older couples who mentor almost always find it an enriching experience for their own marriage. [For information, see *The Marriage Mentor Manual* (Zondervan Publishing House) in which the Parrotts give specific guidance for setting up such a program.]

Oddsmakers say the chances are 5 in 10 that a marriage will end in divorce. If one or both partners are still teenagers, they say the odds for divorce are even higher. If either partner witnessed an unhappy marriage at home, the odds increase again. If one or both partners come from broken homes, the odds rise still higher. If either partner has been divorced, the odds soar. If there has been regular sexual involvement before marriage, or if either or both partners abuse alcohol or drugs, the odds skyrocket.

Regardless of contemporary couples' odds, I believe there is much that ministers and laypeople alike can do to help couples beat them. My prayer is that in spite of the daunting statistics, a new generation of couples will go back to square one and learn the rudiments of lifelong marriage. My prayer is that we will save this generation's marriages before they even begin.

Questions for Reflection

- Why do you think so few engaged couples seek any kind of professional help from a minister or a counselor before they get married?
- On a personal note, what do you believe is the most important skill newlyweds need to learn if their love is to go the distance?
- Many believe the only way to ensure that couples get the preparation they need for marriage is to have ministers in a community agree that they will not marry a couple unless they have met the agreed-upon preparation requirements. What do you think of this?
- Have you considered mentoring a younger couple who is just starting out? How do you think this might benefit them as well as you?

Singles Need Fellowship, Support, and Ministry

Many married people have difficulty believing anyone wants to be single. These people assume that persons choosing singleness have something wrong with them. One woman told me that when a woman remains single, "Some people think nobody wants to marry her, but they don't realize that's the way she wants to be, or maybe she'll get married later." A single adult director said the biggest misconception she came across about never-married adults is "they are constantly looking for a mate. That is a most untrue statement. They're looking for a support group, a fellowship, a body of believers. Many people think the only reason single adults go to a single adult group is to find a mate." She pointed out that evaluations showed the spiritual aspects concerned them most. "They came expecting Christian fellowship and spiritual bonding, and that's what they found." Some find a Christian mate through single adult groups, but it is unwise for leaders to plan their activities with the assumption they are running a Christian dating service. This turns off many single adults faster than anything else. Linda LeSourd states, "Single groups are usually heavily conditioned toward marriage, and thus perpetuate the myth that marriage is the ultimate solution to all one's problems. Frequently, they are characterized by a heavy dating emphasis which fosters game-playing and superficiality in relationships, especially between men and women." Single adults should make dating decisions on their own without activities that center on making them into couples.[1]

Joe Bentz

9

Singles Have Families Too

It is possible for everyone to find the deepest unity of heart and soul without marriage.

—Heini Arnold

TERRY LIVES ALONE. HE IS SINGLE, 34 YEARS OLD, AND HAS NEVER married. He lives and works downtown in an architectural firm. Terry has many friends and is actively involved in his church. He isn't gay, weird, a social misfit, or tied to his parents' apron strings. At one point he was engaged to be married, but his fiancé broke it off. Someday Terry may get married, but for now he lives by himself in a studio apartment.

Terry is one of a growing number of adults in our society whom we classify as being single. The truth is that all of us start our adult lives as single. Nearly all of us date, court, and marry. Of those who ultimately marry, about one-half return to singlehood through divorce. Among those who remain married, half return to singlehood when their spouse dies. Singlehood is thus a very important part of the average person's experience, whether during young adulthood, middle age, old age, or any combination of these life stages.

In spite of its importance, we give relatively little attention to being single—even in the Church. Consider the irony: Our faith is built on a Jewish single adult from Galilee whose ministry was preceded by a single adult named John the Baptist and whose mission thrust was first modeled by a single adult named Paul. Yet, relatively speaking, few of today's churches are paying a great deal of attention to the 68 million unmarried adults in the United States.

The number of single adults is rising as a result of several factors. To begin with, marriage is being delayed by more and more people, and the longer they postpone marriage, the more likely they are to remain single. It is now estimated that nearly 10 percent of men and women in their 20s today will never marry.[1] Increased rates of divorce and decreased likelihood of remarriage account for a good portion of singles as well. Whatever the reasons, we can no longer ignore this important segment of our society. Singles are here to stay, and their numbers are growing.

Who Are the Single Adults?

Arthur Shotak has divided singles into four types: (1) *Ambivalents* are voluntarily single and consider their singleness temporary. They are not seeking marital partners, but they are open to the idea of marriage. (2) *Wishfuls* are involuntarily and temporarily single. They are actively seeking marital partners but have not found a mate yet. (3) *Resolveds* are individuals who regard themselves as permanently single. (4) *Regretfuls* are singles who would prefer to marry but are resigned to their fate. A large number of these are well-educated, high-earning women over 40 who find a shortage of similar men a result of the marriage gradient.

Whatever the classification of a particular single person, however, all are part of a family—the family of origin with siblings, parents, grandparents, and many other relatives. Singles' family life may be different from those who live with other family members, but the familial part of life is important to most single adults. In fact, research has found that single adults are creative in the ways they invent familylike conditions. They often develop friendships that are "almost family" in varying ways. Also, many singles find social organizations in their neighborhoods or where they work that help meet the needs the family realm meets. And, of course, many singles enjoy the benefits of being part of the family of God.

The Church family has the same Father, and we know that all believers are adopted into God's family (John 1:12-13; Gal. 4:4-7; Eph. 1:5). And depending on where a single person attends church, he or she can feel acceptance, encouragement, and love with others in the congregation. This experience for the single Christian, however, can vary greatly from church to church—which brings up the issue of what the Church can do to nurture the single person in the family of God.

What the Church Can Do for Single People

In a helpful article titled "Beyond the Ark Syndrome," Harold Smith points out that the Early Church of Acts (see Acts 6) faced a dilemma centering around singles.[2] They broached the situation as an opportunity, and their response can serve as a model for us. First, they faced the problem head-on. They acknowledged that a segment in the Church—the widows—were being overlooked. This is a far more healthful approach than denying even the possibility of neglect and labeling singles as "crybabies."

Second, they listened. They got the disciples together and hashed out the issue. Church leaders need to ask the single adults in their midst, "What is it like to be a single adult in this culture? What is it like to be a single adult in this church?"

Third, they were honest about their feelings. They admitted their fear that "the ministry of the [W]ord" might be neglected if time and energy had to be diverted to serving these singles. Candidly admitting such reservations is the first step toward finding solutions.

Fourth, they considered alternatives. There were none for the Early Church—no government assistance for widows.

There are no *acceptable* alternatives for today's Church either, where singles are concerned. Think about it: If the church does not aggressively reach single adults, who in your community will do so? Singles' bars? New Age cults?

Fifth, they acted. The Early Church chose seven of their best people and commissioned them to serve the widows. Today's churches need to do likewise, seeking out highly capable people for singles' ministry and providing ongoing training to keep them effective.

The message that singles are second-class citizens is communicated in subtle ways in our modern churches. Are potluck tables set for sixes and eights, or for fives and sevens? When was the last time you heard a sermon illustration that featured a single adult? When was the last time you invited a single adult to join you for dinner after church? As Smith puts it, "The loneliest point of the entire week for many single adults is noon on Sunday."

If you are reading this chapter as a single person, I hope you will forgive our egocentrism when it emerges. And if you are not single, I hope you will consider ways in which you can broaden your horizon by being more inclusive of singles in the family of God. As Reuben Welch might say, we really do need each other.

Before concluding this chapter, let us note one more observation—singleness is sometimes a special call.

A Special Call for Some

It is a mistake to assume that singleness is simply a transitional period for all singles. It is not. Some have a special call of God to a single life. Jesus declared that there were those who were single "for the sake of the kingdom of heaven" (Matt. 19:12, NASB). And Paul builds on this foundation by suggesting that the unmarried can focus their energies toward the work of God in a way that the married simply cannot (1 Cor. 7:32-35).

Some have misunderstood Paul for urging people to seriously consider the single life, but the truth is that his words are filled with practical wisdom. He was not against marriage—in fact, he compares the union couples enjoy in marriage to the union of Christ and His Church (Eph. 5:22-32). But Paul did insist that we count the cost. You see, no one should enter the covenant of marriage without realizing the immense time and energy required to make that relationship work. "The unmarried man is anxious about the affairs of the Lord, how to please the Lord; but the married man is anxious about worldly affairs, how to please his wife, and his interests are divided" (1 Cor. 7:32-34, RSV).

In the Christian family, therefore, not only must we make room for singles, but we must honor the vocational celibate who has chosen a single life in order to focus his or her energies more narrowly on the service of the kingdom of God. Jesus himself is an example of this, as is Paul. This lifestyle, of course, is neither inferior or superior; it is simply a different calling.

To the wishful single I would like to speak words of trust and hope. God is still sovereign, no matter what the frustration of our life may indicate. He can bring about wonderful things for you in your relationships. Trust Him, do all you can yourself, and live in hope. And even if marriage does not come, you can know that His grace is sufficient even for that.

Questions for Reflection
- During colonial times singles were penalized by higher taxes, presumably to encourage marriages. How do we still penalize singles in our society?
- This chapter classified several different types of singles (for example, "ambivalents," "wishfuls," "resolveds," and "regretfuls"). Which do you see as most common?
- What are you doing in your local congregation to include singles in the church family?

Hers, Mine, and All Ours

Here's a story of a lovely lady
Who was busy raising three kids of her own . . .

Our name doesn't rhyme with "lady," but when friends and strangers see Amy and me out and about with our six kids—hers, mine, ours, and "all ours"—they love to describe us as a '90s version of the Bradys.

We definitely meet all the criteria of a blended family. Somehow in the blending process we haven't gotten too mixed up. We've had to face some challenges of pulling our family together when certain dynamics would push us apart, but we've discovered the full range of joys—even a few extras—found in a nuclear family.

Amy and I have discovered that when we dedicate our marriage and children to God—not just in a onetime ceremony at the front of the sanctuary, but as a daily prayer—He helps us do what we can't do by ourselves. Our six kids truly love each other. They miss one another during absences. They like being part of a big family, where even dinner is an event. They can fight like cats and dogs one minute, but they also defend one another against outsiders. They're kind to each other. They entertain each other to the point that sometimes Amy and I believe it's easier having six kids than one.

Because Amy and I know divorce is not part of God's best plan, we realize we must rely even more on Him to transform something painful into something beautiful for both us and the kids. The reality is that all parents—whether always happily married or divorced—must put their children into the hands of God. Our divorces made that reality become more urgent.

A "hers, mine, and ours" household does present challenges that won't go away, but the good news is that a wonderful family life is possible. We may not be the Bradys, but we wouldn't trade what we have for the world.

Mark Gilroy

10

Blended Families and Parents Without Partners

*The family is our refuge and springboard;
nourished on it, we can advance to new
horizons. In every conceivable manner, the
family is link to our past, bridge to our future.*

—**Alex Haley**

DIVORCE OR DEATH ENDS A MARRIAGE BUT NOT A FAMILY. THE family reorganizes itself into what researchers are beginning to call the "binuclear family." This family is a nuclear family divided in two—where the husband/wife relationship is dissolved but not the father/mother, mother/child, or father/child relationship.

Over one-fifth of all families are currently single-parent families. They are the fastest-growing family form in the United States. The single-parent family, more than the dual-worker family or stepfamily, is a radical departure from the traditional nuclear model, which includes two parents. No other family type has increased in number as rapidly. Approximately half of all children born in the 1990s live in single-parent families sometime during their childhoods. And 87 percent of single-parent families are headed by women.

Blended families are also on the rise. "As soon as the ink was dry on the divorce papers, they both remarried," Jenny told me in a counseling session. "Within a period of two days, I gained seven new stepbrothers and stepsisters." It took Jenny's parents five years to finalize the divorce, but it took only an instant for Jenny to have a radically new family. And she's not alone. It is predicted that by 2000 there will be more stepfamilies in America than any other family form. If we care about families, we need to understand and support blended families and parents without partners.

How Single Parenting Is Different

After a divorce, the single parent is usually glad to have the children with him or her. Everything else seems to have fallen apart, but as long as divorced parents have their children, they retain their parental function. Their children's need for them reassures them of their own importance. The mother's success as a parent becomes even more important to counteract the feelings of low self-esteem that result from divorce. Feeling depressed, the mother knows she must bounce back for the children. Yet after a short period, she comes to realize that her children do not fill the void caused by her divorce. The children are a chore as well as a pleasure, and she may resent being constantly tied down by their needs. Thus, minor incidents with the children—refusal to eat or a temper tantrum—may get blown out of proportion.

A single-parent family is not the same as a two-parent family with one parent temporarily absent. The permanent absence of one parent dramatically changes the way in which the parenting adult relates to the children. Generally, the mother becomes closer and more responsive to her children. Her authority role changes too. A greater distinction between parents and children exists in two-parent homes. Rules are developed by both mothers and fathers. Parents generally have an implicit understanding that they will back each other up in child-rearing matters and enforce mutually agreed-on rules. In the single-parent family no other partner is available to help maintain such agreements; as a result, the children may find themselves in a much more egalitarian situation. Consequently, they have more power to negotiate rules. They can badger a single parent into getting their way about staying up late, watching television, or going out. Any parent who has tried to get children to do something they do not want to do knows how soon he or she (the parent) can be worn down. So single parents are more willing to compromise or give in. In this way, children acquire considerable decision-making power in single-parent homes. They gain it through default—the single parent finds it too difficult to argue with them all the time.

Children in single-parent homes may also learn more responsibility. They may learn to help with kitchen chores, to clean up their messes, or to be more considerate. In the single-parent home, the children are encouraged to recognize the work their parent does and the importance of cooperation. One single mom told me that before the divorce her husband had always washed the dishes. At that time it had been difficult to get the children to help around the house. Now, she said, the children pitch in to help with the dishes, vacuuming, and other things that need to be done.

In spite of some positives that can emerge in single parenting, the struggles are glaring. A review of relevant studies on children from single-parent households found that they tend not to do as well academically as those from two-parent families. They are also more likely to drop out of high school. These kids in general marry younger, have children earlier, and are also more prone to divorce. Single-parent families certainly need our prayers.

Blended Families

Satirist Art Buchwald calls blended families "tangled families." He may be close to the truth in some cases. When persons enter a stepfamily, they expect to re-create a family identical to an intact family. The intact nuclear family becomes the model against which they judge their successes and failures. But researchers believe that stepfamilies are significantly different from intact families.[1] Several structural characteristics make the stepfamily different from the traditional first-marriage family, and each is laden with potential difficulties.

- In blended families, almost all members have lost an important primary relationship. The children may mourn the loss of their parent or parents, and the spouses of the loss of their former mates. Because of this, anger is sometimes displaced onto the new stepparent.

- One biological parent lives outside the current family. He or she may either support or interfere with the new family. Power struggles may occur between the absent parent and the custodial parent, and there may be jealousy between the absent parent and the stepparent.

- The relationship between a parent and his or her children predates the relationship between the new partners. Children have often spent considerable time in a single-parent family structure. They have formed close and different bonds with their parent. A new husband or wife may seem to be an interloper interfering in the children's special relationship with their parent. A new stepparent may find that he or she must compete with the children for their parent's attention.

- Stepparent roles are ill defined. No one knows quite what he or she is supposed to do as a stepparent. Most stepparents try role after role until they find one that fits.

- Many children in stepfamilies are also members of the noncustodial parent's household. Each home may have different rules and expectations. When conflict arises, children may try to play one household against the other.

- Children in stepfamilies have at least one extra pair of

grandparents. Children get a new set of stepgrandparents, but the role these new grandparents are to play is usually not clear.

In spite of many hurdles, the overwhelming majority of stepfamilies come to feel that they have become "family." When asked how they have done this, most reply by saying that they have developed a sense of connectedness and a mutual feeling of caring and support. In creating their new family, stepfamilies begin to see themselves as uniquely different from all other families. And in doing so, stepfamilies become families in a very profound sense.

Grace for Single Parents and Blended Families

Let's face it: life for any family is not easy. As families navigate the waters of life, storms are inevitable. And for some families, those storms bring an unpredictable upheaval where it seems, at least for a time, that the course has been lost. But families—single-parent, blended, and otherwise—who navigate with God at the helm will not sink. They will find strength to persevere.

In spite of our weakness, we need to keep in mind that God remains all the things we are not. Since this is true, He can and will give us everything we lack when the unexpected hits us head-on.

The cries of the single parent and the stepparent are sometimes left unaddressed by the Church. Yet how sad to avoid ministering grace to places where it is often needed the most! I was fortunate to be raised in a stable family who never encountered the unforeseen squalls resulting in a break. And I have been blessed in my 12-year marriage to enjoy the fulfillment of a loving partner. But I consider some words penned by George Washington Carver when I think about those who did not make it through the storms successfully: "How far you go in life depends on your being tender with the young, compassionate with the aged, sympathetic with the striving, and tolerant of the weak and the strong. Because someday in life you will have been all of these." How true! No matter what condition our family is in, we need the grace of God as desperately as any other.

According to Rom. 8:28, "All things work together for good to them that love God, to them who are the called according to his purpose" (KJV). Loving God means finding ways to apply grace and understanding in difficult family transitions—whether that be in our own family or of the families around us.

Questions for Reflection

- Take a moment to put yourself in the shoes of someone who is a suddenly single parent. What goes through your mind? What challenges are you immediately faced with?
- Do the same for the child who has suddenly had a drastic change in his or her family structure. What do you experience as you empathize with this child?
- In what specific, concrete ways can the Church administer grace to single-parent and blended families?

Equipping Families in the Local Church

"Strong families contribute to strong churches, and strong churches contribute to strong families." The principle is a simple one to proclaim, but a more difficult one to practice, because in reality, many churches drain energy from the family, and many family activities end up draining life from the church. Here are three surefire suggestions that can help the local church maintain the balance:

1. *Model the priority of families in the congregation.* Intentionally include families in times of corporate worship, education, compassionate ministry, and social activities. Don't eliminate age-level and gender-specific ministries, but do schedule enough integrated services and activities to demonstrate that families are important.

2. *Offer educational opportunities that equip marriage partners and parents to function more effectively in their roles.* Don't focus on gloom and guilt—it's too easy to focus on all that's wrong with marraiges and families these days. Focus on enablement and encouragement as a means of strengthening family systems. Concentrate on some of the basic skills necessary for effective relationships.

3. *Equip families to live "Christianly" at home.* Many contemporary families need assistance in reframing the worship experience to fit into a busy, sometimes disconnected lifestyle. Encourage families to celebrate events on the Christian calendar and ordinary times by providing ideas for celebrations and devotionals for the seasons as a way of introducing families to worship in the home.

There's no need to force a choice between church life and family life. If each works to strengthen the other, both come out ahead, and ultimately the message of the gospel is more effectively modeled at church and at home.

Ed Robinson

11

Godly Kids in "a House Divided"?

Bring them [your children] up in the
training and instruction of the Lord.
—Eph. 6:4

MARILYN'S HUSBAND, JIM, HAS NEVER BEEN ONE TO GO TO church. He sometimes says he thinks God doesn't exist. While both Marilyn and Jim grew up in Christian homes, they strayed away from the church as teenagers. Shortly after the birth of their first child, however, Marilyn began attending church again. She joined a women's Bible study and in the process renewed her personal commitment to Christ. Jim, on the other hand, was reluctant. Sometimes he wanted nothing to do with "that religious stuff," as he called it. He didn't try to prevent Marilyn from going to church and taking the kids, but he had decided church wasn't for him. He could get along just as well without it.

Marilyn and Jim's story is not all that uncommon. There are plenty of couples who are "unequally yoked" (2 Cor. 6:14, KJV). Common or not, however, the relationship is often hard and sometimes heartbreaking. After all, raising a moral child with biblical values in the crosscurrents of today's world requires its own brand of courage and wisdom. Surveys report that 61 percent of high school students cheat on exams, and 33 percent shoplift. Nearly half do not know the meaning of abstinence or chastity, let alone practicing them from conviction. There is no need to state the statistics on drug and alcohol abuse, since they increase daily. At times it seems we are raising a nation of moral illiterates.

"There's no mystery why young people are turning to drugs, alcohol, sex, and delinquency," according to Paul Lewis, president of Family University. "They don't have sufficient contact with mature adults to have feedback and correction. So many of them develop the perception that their choices don't have consequences, that life is lived by fate or luck of the draw."

This moral decline among youngsters has led to the emergence of several books and articles with imposing titles like *The War Against the Family*, *The De-Valuing of America*, and *The Family Under Siege*, just to name a few. Most experts agree that moms and dads today face more parenting hurdles in raising children with Christian values than ever before. But on top of what sometimes feels like insurmountable odds, some courageous parents have the added dimension of trying to build Christian character in their children in spite of having a partner who does not possess a personal faith.

When *Christian Parenting* magazine asked readers about this difficult parenting in spiritually divided families, dozens replied (all women). Judy Kasel wrote, "I have been married for 17 years. I was born again 3 months after our marriage. My spouse is still not a Christian." Leanne Ozcel wrote, "I am a mother of a 3-year-old boy and a 1-year-old girl . . . My husband will not have family devotions nor will he attend church with us. He also didn't want our children to be baptized. [I try] to instill Christian values during the day while my non-Christian spouse goes to work." Marjorie Cavender wrote, "Nobody can imagine what it is like to live with an unsaved spouse unless you've actually been there. I have been married 11 years and have been praying all of this time for my husband to come to know the Lord." Nancy Kennedy wrote, "I've spent the past 17 out of 20 years bringing my children to church by myself and I've had to deal with the questions: 'Why doesn't Dad go to church with us?' and 'Will Dad go to heaven when he dies?' As the kids got older, the questions became more probing: 'Why doesn't God answer our prayers?' and 'Why does God allow our family to be the way it is?'"

The struggles faced by parents like these are innumerable and often neglected in the roster of local church concerns. As one reader put it, "So much is written to single parents. We who have children to raise and a non-Christian spouse to contend with need support too."

It's a valid point. How can you give your children a godly upbringing when your spouse isn't a Christian? What should you tell your kids when they ask why Dad doesn't go to church or doesn't say grace or bedtime prayers? Little has been written for parents in this predicament. And when it is addressed, it is often relegated to theological perspectives on being "unequally yoked." Few practical, doable solutions are offered. This chapter, however, is an attempt to reverse that trend.

What You Can Do

You have probably heard that old truisms become clichés because they are so accurate: "Monkey see; monkey do." "The apple doesn't fall far from the tree." "Actions speak louder than words." "Spare the rod and spoil the child." These old one-liners about raising children certainly have current validity. But putting aside the clichés, many determined readers of *Christian Parenting* offered specific advice to parents who are not married to a Christian spouse. There were dozens of helpful suggestions, and here are some of their most effective solutions:

Respect your spouse. "Mutual respect" is the agreed-upon starting place, according to most of the parents who wrote in. It seems that while disagreeing with and debating a spouse's worldview is tempting, most of these parents have learned from experience that punching holes in a partner's belief system does not flood the problem with fresh air. "It is critically important to show my husband respect," one woman said. "If I don't respect him as a person, how can I expect my children to respect their father?" Sure, you might want to point out what he is missing by not accepting Christ, but these kinds of messages are better heard when they come from a foundation of respect. The main point, however, is that if you show respect to your partner, you are much more likely to get respect back from him. As Henry Ward Beecher once said, "If you want someone to see what Christ will do for him, let him see what Christ has done for you." Your husband is far more likely to be open about faith issues if he knows you are not setting him up to look or feel foolish. To build this kind of foundation, you may want to take a moment to make a list of qualities you respect about your husband. What characteristics in him do you admire and want your children to emulate? You may also want to think about how you show your husband that you respect him. To take this exercise a step farther, ask yourself how your partner would answer this same question.

Build your marital bond. Another common solution for dealing with the spiritually divided home focuses on modeling a healthy marriage. It seems most agree with the adage that says the best thing a mom can do for her children is to love her husband. Laurie Wyatt writes, "I have found it crucial to foster a unified and respectful relationship with my unchristian spouse. While my children and I remain very active in our local church, we give Daddy first priority in time and hugs and communication." This kind of love and respect is vitally important to your children. Of course, they may question Daddy's absence in church, but that does not open the door for you to criticize his behavior. It is, in fact, an opportunity to let your children know how much you love and respect your husband. "If the children question their father's reluctance to participate in spiritual activities," writes Laurie, "I explain that each individual has his own timing and style when it comes to a relationship with the Lord." Building your marriage and loving your husband—in spite of his lack of faith—is truly one of the best things you can do for your children.

Find common ground. Even though your partner's lack of personal faith creates a spiritual gap in your relationship, you still have much in common. And when it comes to what both of you want for your children, it is important to recognize your common ground. If you have lost sight of this shared vision, take time to rediscover it. Talk about what values you want your children to embody. What principles do you both want them to live by? If you are like most couples, you agree on many of the basics even if your partner doesn't put the principles in a Christian context. Next, talk about how the two of you will teach these values and principles to your children. This is generally where the rubber meets the road. It may be that your non-Christian spouse is likely to agree that your children can learn "good" principles at church even if he or she (your spouse) doesn't agree with the theological basis. The bottom line is that the two of you must find common ground in how you want your children to live. Once this is established, you can attempt other solutions.

Teach what you believe. Researchers estimate that the average child asks 500,000 questions by the age of 15. And many of them are "why" and "how" questions that can lead to spiritual lessons. That is nearly half a million opportunities to let your child know how you think and what you believe about God. It is not enough to relegate spiritual lessons to Sunday School teachers and pastors. God gives every child a special sensitivity to His presence and His handiwork in creation. And a child grows spiritually when you associate God with life around him or her. So while your partner may not join you in your godly explanations, there are countless one-on-one opportunities to teach your child godly ways. This is not a technique for going behind your partner's back; it's a way of living out your convictions. It is a way of being you. Parents today, broadly speaking, are more hesitant and insecure about their authority role. For whatever reason, they are less likely than previous generations of parents to stand firm. But as a Christian parent, you don't have to follow the herd. So heed the advice of others in your shoes, and don't be afraid to teach what you believe.

Be an example of Christian living. The Bible says, "Train up a child in the way he should go: and when he is old, he will not depart from it" (Prov. 22:6, KJV). It is true that guidance is often given through instruction, but life's greatest lessons are taught through example. Not the kind of examples that overtly say, "Here—let me show you how it's done," or "See? We go to church," but in the thoughtless moments when life is at full throttle. It's during the daily grind, when someone cuts you off in traffic or when your checkbook doesn't balance, that your child is learning some of life's most important lessons. He or she is quietly, almost unconsciously, observing how you react and how you feel. Sir Thomas Fuller said, "A good example is the best sermon." So while the temptation is to focus on what your children are picking up from their non-Christian parent, a more important concern is what they are picking up from *you.* Richard Baxter, a famous English pastor, preached passionately for three years without any visible results. In desperation one day he threw himself across the floor of his study and cried out, "God, You must do something with these people."

He later wrote that God spoke to him that day and said, "Baxter, you're working in the wrong place. You expect revival to come to these people. First, focus on you." That's pretty good advice for the parent whose spouse isn't a Christian.

Steer clear of guilt. "Is it remotely possible that any other parents in any other age have had the opportunity to feel guilty in as many ways as we have?" asks Glen Collins in *How to Be a Guilty Parent.* "Did they have PG movies? Dinky Donuts breakfast cereal? Video games at the checkout counter?" Parental guilt these days runs rampant. And for the parent in your predicament, it is all the more consuming. Do you ever feel responsible for your partner's lack of faith; that somehow, someway, if you could just do or be something different, he or she would become a Christian? Don't pummel yourself with needless guilt feelings. Self-punishment will do nothing but undermine your capacity to be who you really are—a child of God, freely forgiven. If the truth be known, if you do not recognize and resolve your feelings of guilt, if you do not rely on God's grace, you will end up projecting feelings of guilt onto your children and your partner. Nothing could be worse, for guilt cuts the heart out of a healthy home. So many strands of hope and fear, of ardent wishes and anxious apprehensions, are tangled together in the ties that bind parents and child. But to maintain a healthy connection, the strand of guilt must be kept from strangling parental love.

Pray for your spouse and children. I would be remiss if I did not mention a solution that appeared in nearly every single letter—prayer. Denise High, a working mother with two toddlers and a husband who is not a Christian, is typical: "Our diverging spiritual paths greatly affect our relationship, and my answer has been found in a four-letter word: PRAY. I 'pray without ceasing' that my spouse will be filled with questions for which only God has answers; that our children will be drawn to the Lord; and that I will be strengthened and guided to be a good Christian role model for our family." Prayer in its simplest definition is merely a wish turned Godward. And according to George MacDonald, "Anything large enough for a wish to light upon is large enough to hang a prayer on." So turn your wishes toward God. Raise your thoughts to heaven.

Don't Quit

Pastor Charles Swindoll says every family with children is a cross between Grand Central Station and the Indianapolis 500. Comedian Martin Mull says, "Having children is like having a bowling alley installed in your head." Parenting, no matter how you look at it, is tough work. So don't give up hope; don't quit. In spite of obstacles, you can raise your kids on a godly path.

In his excellent book *Family Shock,* Gary Collins tells a story that has a message for every parent trying to raise godly children without a Christian spouse. It is about Ignacy Paderewski, the great Polish pianist, composer, and statesman. He was waiting to begin one of his recitals when an eight-year-old boy from the audience slid out of his seat and headed for the stage before his parents could stop him. The young man seated himself at the piano and began playing "Chopsticks." The audience scowled at this brash lad with his jarring sounds. From the side of the stage, however, Paderewski entered and quietly slid up behind the boy, reaching his long arms out to the right and left of the two small hands. Paderewski began to improvise on the "Chopsticks" theme. Suddenly the simple melody, played imperfectly, took on a sound of beauty, blessed with the master's approval and touch. The audience burst into applause. Everybody noticed that Paderewski kept whispering into the boy's ear. It was later revealed that he just kept saying, "Don't quit. Don't quit."

If you are in this parenting predicament, you may often feel alone and even hopeless. But don't give up hope. Listen to the Master whispering in your ear, "Don't quit. Don't quit."

Questions for Reflection
- Why do you think some spouses want nothing to do with religion even when the person they love more than anyone else is vitally involved in the life of the church?
- What advice would you give to a parent who is married to a nonbeliever? Do you agree that it is best to stay clear of the guilt trap?
- What can the church family do to help parents who are unequally yoked? What can the church family do to help the children from these families?

Making Time for God in a Busy Family

The Bible is a book about family—God's family, our family. It is a story of the relationships we have with each other as brothers and sisters, mothers and fathers, sons and daughters. It is a story of the relationship we have with God our Father, Jesus Christ our Brother, and the Holy Spirit our Guide. It is a story of relationships in progress, constantly changing and ever growing. It is a story of the way faith shapes and strengthens these relationships.

Faith and family are the threads of our life. Separately the threads will become worn and will eventually break under the pressures. Together they form the rope that holds firm against the storms of life.

Our families have shaped our faith, and our faith is continually shaping our families. The two are woven together side by side. The world tries with all its might to separate our families from our faith, but we must resist these constant pulls. How our faith shapes our families will affect how the next generation allows their faith to then shape their families, and so on, and so on.

Fred Fullerton

12

Families and the Faith

*A church within a church, a republic
within a republic, a world within a world,
is spelled in four letters: HOME. If things
go right there, they go right everywhere.
The doorsill of the dwelling house is the
foundation of the Church.*

—DeWitt Talmage

FROM THE BEGINNING, SINCE ADAM AND EVE SAT AROUND THE first family dining table and bowed their heads for grace, there has been a marriage of sorts between faith and family. After all, Adam and Eve were the handiwork of God. And even after their fall, they were a worshiping family. The first murder occurred over differences in sacrifices and the jealousy the inequity generated. The relationship of faith and family has not always been easy, not even today. However, the marriage of family and faith is still identified as a major goal in many homes worldwide.

The gold-and-silver thread of family and faith runs through the Bible like a beautiful cord of love, forever identifying the way for family and religion to fortify each other. Abraham and Sarah headed a family dynasty that endured for 38 chapters in Genesis, 12 to 50, and covered four generations in 360 years, 2166 B.C. to 1806 B.C. Faith in God was the centerpiece in the religious life of their family and in the families of their son Isaac, grandson Jacob, and great-grandson Joseph. Their stories are held together by that unbroken gold and silver thread of family and faith.

Moses survived a death edict against all Jewish babies because of a close-knit family who worked together to carry out God's rescue strategy, beginning in the bulrushes and ending in Pharaoh's palace. And when Moses delivered the children of Israel out of Egypt, he rescued them as *families,* including those for whom travel was a struggle, such as the infirmed, the very young, the maimed, pregnant women, even the insolent. But from the beginning the Hebrews in Egypt, on the Sinai Desert, and in the Promised Land were a nation of people known for their solidarity in family and faith. Even today Jewish families carry the banner for strong relationships with each other in the family and with the synagogue.

The genealogy of Jesus, as presented by both Matthew and Luke, is a generational report on families of faith who prepared the biological way for the birth of Jesus.

Paul used the metaphor of the Church and Christ's unconditional love for it to describe how men ought to love their wives (Eph. 5). And he used one of the Ten Commandments—"Honour thy father and thy mother" (Exod. 20:12, KJV)—to explain why it is right for children to obey their parents (Eph. 6). "Faith," "obedience," "love," and "submission" are good words in both church and home.

Even salvation statements in the Bible often link faith and family. Joshua married faith and family in his covenant renewal statement: "As for me and my household, we will serve the LORD" (Josh. 24:15). Luke accounts for the family faith of Cornelius: "A centurion in what was known as the Italian Regiment. He and all his family were devout and God-fearing" (Acts 10:1-2). Martha, Mary, and Lazarus loved Jesus and opened their home of single adults to Him. Paul affirmed the faith of Timothy, which was passed from his grandmother Lois to his mother, Eunice, and then to Timothy (2 Tim. 1:5). Paul included the family in his salvation statement to the Philippian jailer: "Believe in the Lord Jesus, and you will be saved—you and your household" (Acts 16:31). And even in the Trinity, Christ does not call God "King." He called Him "Father." Faith and religion are a family thing, and the dynamics of the family are a metaphor for both.

Faith and family need to be understood for what they are. Faith is not a parachute for rescuing us, but a gyroscope for keeping us on course. Religion includes faith, but faith by itself is not religion—it is a relationship. Christian faith is trust in God through Jesus Christ, God's Son, kept alive by the comforting, abiding presence of the Holy Spirit.

Faith is often connected to human feelings or emotions, but not necessarily. It is a decision for commitment. And a commitment of faith is the foundation for building a relationship. This is true both in our religion and in our family. Our faith is in God, His Son Jesus, and in the Holy Spirit, as well as His Word. But faith is also expressed toward members of our family. Without trust, no family relationships can endure. As God forgives us, we forgive each other. God does not forgive us because we deserve forgiveness, but because He loves and sees us as members of the family. And we forgive each other within the family for the same reasons. We love each other and forgive each other because we are family. As we enjoy God's presence, so we enjoy the presence of the family we trust. The longer the relationship lives, the sweeter it grows. Years deepen, brighten, and enhance a relationship of faith, both toward God and toward each other within the family.

The Silent Bells Ring Out for Faith

When the Second Continental Congress of the American colonies realized, after the battles of Lexington and Concord, that reconciliation with Great Britain was fading fast, they debated the issues and then appointed Thomas Jefferson and a committee to write a document that declared their independence. After two weeks of writing and with minor changes by Benjamin Franklin and John Adams, they signed it—all 56 members.

Several belligerent expressions of freedom were expressed in the process, including John Hancock's signature, which was large enough for King George III to read without his spectacles. But the most dramatic signal for freedom came in the ringing of the Liberty Bell. Today the bell is cracked, a relic that will not ring but is still revered as a silent voice of freedom. It is enshrined for millions to see with this silent message from the Bible engraved across its face: *"Proclaim liberty throughout all the land unto all the inhabitants thereof"* (Lev. 25:10, KJV).

When it comes to spiritual liberty in the family, there are three silent bells with the words "faith," "hope," and "love" written across the face of each:

Faith is renewed in a daily quiet time alone with God. This is what Paul had in mind when he said, "Be not conformed to this world: but be ye transformed by the renewing of your mind" (Rom. 12:2, KJV). The mind is the place of residence for our attitudes, our habitual ways of looking at life, and our mind-set. It is also the central power station for making the flow of decisions that dominate our behavior. That mind needs renewing every day. This is that mind that sets us free by faith or holds us captive by our own doubts. And the best way to renew the faith that resides in the mind is to open it daily to the fresh air of God's Word, a time of quietly listening to the voice of the Holy Spirit or simply to enjoy His abiding presence. These lofty experiences can be achieved only through the discipline of a daily quiet time. Faith proves itself in the skirmishes of life, but it grows in the quiet times of the soul.

Hope is the family flower that blossoms in times of united devotions. Hope is sanctified optimism. Hope is the lens that helps couples and children to see the possibilities in each other. Hope is never based on where we are, but where we may one day be; not on what we are, but who we may become.

Family times for devotional thoughts and hearthside prayers are hard to come by. Those times will never just happen. They require leadership on someone's part. In the Trinity, leadership comes from the Father; but among earthly families, leadership in family worship often comes through the spiritual sensitivities of the mother.

Any time can be selected for the family gathering, but the easiest is probably during the family's most important meal of the day. The format is as open as the sky above. But it must be tied to realities appreciated by members of the family. Family worship is not discipline time or lecture time or an opportunity to clear the air over unresolved piques among family members. And family prayers are self-defeating if they are distorted as means for getting at individual members. Some appropriate approaches to family worship include prayer requests, individual comments, scripture, and singing. During this spiritual exercise, hope will come alive even when it is unseen and unfelt. Family solidarity, personal sensitivity to each other, divine worship, and mental notes for relational follow-up are all part of the hope that family worship encourages.

And finally, "church" is the word we use to describe the Body of Christ, in which family members receive additional training in faith toward God and with each other.

The cause-and-effect sequence in choosing a church are often inadequate and faulted. A big choir, beautiful building, and proximity to home are secondary reasons of choice. More important to a family of faith are such matters as belief in Christ as God's Son, commitment to the Bible as God's Word, practices of baptism and Communion, and general spirit and attitude. Every church has a personality, just as each person or each home does. Choosing a church is like choosing a place in which to live. Be careful. Go slowly. Set your standards before you start looking. And once the choice is made, settle in, get involved, and stay the course.

The family of God in the place where you worship is likely to make a big difference in the spiritual life of your family. But accept the fact: no church runs smoothly all the time in every area of Christian service. Every pastor has feet of clay. Pastors are probably challenged with the needs of their own families—maybe overwhelmed. Lay leaders are just that: *lay* leaders. They are the end result of all the things that have ever happened to themselves and to their families. They are still under construction. The church is not a spiritual hothouse designed to produce gilded lilies. It is a garden with a great variety of plants in various stages of growth and dying. And gardens, being what they are, will always tolerate a certain number of weeds. Don't plow up the garden to get at the weeds. Let the oil of the Spirit do His work.

So we have come to the end of our discussion on families and faith. The two are tied together like faith and works. Healthy families are almost always families of faith. But there are no neat formulas. No quick fixes. Not even any shortcuts. Developing a family of faith is a process that calls for leadership in the home, quiet times for individual family members, some kind of continuing family worship, and the care and opportunities of a Christ-centered church with a spiritually sensitive ministry.

By the grace of God we must all do what we can do to strengthen our homes. This is the story of families—yours and mine.

Questions for Reflection

- In the fifth chapter of Ephesians and the first verse of chapter 6, what are three directives Paul gives concerning wives, husbands, and children?
- In what ways do you view faith as a relationship?
- In what ways do you think hope is developed in family worship?
- In your own mind, what is the number one prerequisite for choosing the church where your family will be raised?

Notes

Chapter 1

1. Christopher Buckley, "Profile: You Got a Problem?" *New Yorker,* December 4, 1995, 80-85.

2. A. M. Casale, *Tracking Tomorrow's Trends* (Kansas City: Andrews, McMeel, and Parker).

Chapter 3

1. R. W. Bradley, "Using Sibling Dyads to Understand Career Development," *Personnel and Guidance Journal* 62 (1984): 397-400.

2. E. H. Friedman, *Generation to Generation: Family Process in Church and Synagogue* (New York: Guilford Press, 1985), 34.

Chapter 4

1. Maggie Scarf, *Intimate Worlds: Life Inside the Family* (New York: Random House, 1995).

2. Dolores Curran, *Traits of a Healthy Family* (New York: Ballantine, 1983).

Try This Formula

1. This entire excerpt is from Leola Floren, *The New Boss Has a Milk Mustache* (Kansas City: Beacon Hill Press of Kansas City, 1996), 47.

Family Worship

1. *Conference Minutes* 1:4, cited by John W. Prince, *Wesley on Religious Education* (New York: Methodist Book Concern, 1926), 133. Also see *The Works of John Wesley,* 5:194.

2. This entire "Family Worship" excerpt is from Wesley D. Tracy et al., *The Upward Call* (Kansas City: Beacon Hill Press of Kansas City, 1994), 196-97.

Divorce and Children

1. Judith S. Wallerstein and Sandra Blakeslee, *Second Chances: Men, Women, and Children a Decade After Divorce* (New York: Ticknor and Fields, 1989), 297.

2. George Barna, *The Future of the American Family* (Chicago: Moody Press, 1993), 23.

3. Ibid., 88. Barna cites two telephone surveys of young adults conducted in 1990.

4. Jim Conway, *Adult Children of Legal or Emotional Divorce* (Downers Grove, Ill.: InterVarsity Press, 1990), 28-29.

5. Ibid., 30.

Chapter 7

1. Diane Vaughan, *Uncoupling: Turning Points in Intimate Relationships* (New York: Oxford University Press, 1986).

2. G. Kitson, "Marital Discord and Marital Separation: A County Survey," *Journal of Marriage and the Family* 47 (1985): 693-700.

3. L. Martin Bumpass and J. Sweet, "The Impact of Family Background and Early Marital Factors on Marital Disruption," *Journal of Family Issues* 12 (1991): 22-44.

4. Judith S. Wallerstein, Center for the Family in Transition in Corte Madera, California.

Personal Time with God

1. This entire excerpt is from Grace Ketterman, *Marriage: First Things First* (Kansas City: Beacon Hill Press of Kansas City, 1995), 43-44.

Chapter 8

1. National Center for Health Statistics.

2. Michael McManus, *Marriage Savers* (Grand Rapids: Zondervan Publishing House, 1994).

3. Robert Sternberg, "A Triangular Theory of Love," *Psychological Review* 93 (1986): 119-35.

4. John Gottman, *Why Marriages Succeed or Fail* (New York: Simon and Schuster, 1994).

Singles Need Fellowship, Support, and Ministry

1. This entire excerpt is from Joe Bentz, "A Never-Married Adult's View of the Church," in *The Faces of Single Adult Ministries,* ed. Linda G. Hardin (Kansas City: Beacon Hill Press of Kansas City, 1990), 18.

Chapter 9

1. U.S. Bureau of the Census, Statistical Abstract of the United States, 111th ed. (Washington, D.C.: U.S. Government Printing Office, 1991).

2. Harold Smith, "Beyond the Ark Syndrome: Rethinking Ministry with Single Adults," *Growing Disciples* 2, No. 3 (January—March 1996): 12-19.

Chapter 10

1. Marilyn Coleman and Lawrence Ganong, "The Cultural Stereotyping of Stepfamilies," in *Remarriage and Stepparenting: Current Research and Theory,* ed. Kay Pasley and Marilyn Ihinger-Tallman (New York: Guilford Press, 1987).